The French Have A Word For It

by Georges Feydeau

Translated by Barnett Shaw

From *Le Dindon*

A Samuel French Acting Edition

New York Hollywood London Toronto
SAMUELFRENCH.COM

Copyright © 1983 by Barnett Shaw
LE DINDON by Georges Feydeau Copyright © 1977 by Alain Feydeau
Translated by permission.

ALL RIGHTS RESERVED

CAUTION: Professionals and amateurs are hereby warned that *THE FRENCH HAVE A WORD FOR IT* is subject to a Licensing Fee. It is fully protected under the copyright laws of the United States of America, the British Commonwealth, including Canada, and all other countries of the Copyright Union. All rights, including professional, amateur, motion picture, recitation, lecturing, public reading, radio broadcasting, television and the rights of translation into foreign languages are strictly reserved. In its present form the play is dedicated to the reading public only.

The amateur live stage performance rights to *THE FRENCH HAVE A WORD FOR IT* are controlled exclusively by Samuel French, Inc., and licensing arrangements and performance licenses must be secured well in advance of presentation. PLEASE NOTE that amateur Licensing Fees are set upon application in accordance with your producing circumstances. When applying for a licensing quotation and a performance license please give us the number of performances intended, dates of production, your seating capacity and admission fee. Licensing Fees are payable one week before the opening performance of the play to Samuel French, Inc., at 45 W. 25th Street, New York, NY 10010.

Licensing Fee of the required amount must be paid whether the play is presented for charity or gain and whether or not admission is charged.

Stock licensing fees quoted upon application to Samuel French, Inc.

For all other rights than those stipulated above, apply to: Samuel French, Inc.

Particular emphasis is laid on the question of amateur or professional readings, permission and terms for which must be secured in writing from Samuel French, Inc.

Copying from this book in whole or in part is strictly forbidden by law, and the right of performance is not transferable.

Whenever the play is produced the following notice must appear on all programs, printing and advertising for the play: "Produced by special arrangement with Samuel French, Inc."

Due authorship credit must be given on all programs, printing and advertising for the play.

No one shall commit or authorize any act or omission by which the copyright of, or the right to copyright, this play may be impaired.
No one shall make any changes in this play for the purpose of production.
Publication of this play does not imply availability for performance. Both amateurs and professionals considering a production are strongly advised in their own interests to apply to Samuel French, Inc., for written permission before starting rehearsals, advertising, or booking a theatre.
No part of this book may be reproduced, stored in a retrieval system, or transmitted in any form, by any means, now known or yet to be invented, including mechanical, electronic, photocopying, recording, videotaping, or otherwise, without the prior written permission of the publisher.

ISBN 978-0-573-61886-4   Printed   in   U.S.A.   #8092

THE FRENCH HAVE A WORD FOR IT

CHARACTERS

as they appear:

LUCIENNE VATELIN, *age 25*
EDMOND PONTAGNAC, *a woman chaser, 35*
CREPIN VATELIN, *30, Lucienne's husband*
JEAN, *servant of the Vatelins, any age*
ERNEST REDILLON, *emotional playboy, 32, rather short*
YVONNE PONTAGNAC, *28, wife of Pontagnac*
MARIA, *27, Spanish, wife of Soldignac*
SOLDIGNAC *a French businessman, living in Spain, 30*
ARMANDINE, *19, not too bright lady of the night*
VICTOR, *17, a bellhop at Hotel Ultimus*
MANAGER, *at Hotel Ultimus*
PINCHARD, *55, a medical major in the cavalry*
MADAME PINCHARD (COCO), *50, his wife*
CLARA, *chambermaid at Hotel Ultimus, buxom*
GUEST, *in the hotel*
SECOND GUEST, *in the hotel*
POLICE INSPECTOR DUVAL, *a plainclothes detective*
A GENDARME
POLICE INSPECTOR DUPONT, *another detective*
JEROME, *55, Redillon's unlikely servant*

ACT ONE: A salon in Vatelin's house, Boulevard Chapelle.
ACT TWO: A bedroom in the Hotel Ultimus, Room 39.
ACT THREE: A den in Redillon's bachelor apartment.

THE PLACE: *PARIS.*

THE TIME: *It can be 1900 or thereabouts, but actors should not be burdened with a fashion show. Since there are no dated references in the play, it can be done in a sort of timeless style, both in costumes and settings, without making reference to any definite period. The essential thing is to keep everything energetic and French. But only Maria should speak with a foreign accent.*

THE FRENCH HAVE A WORD FOR IT

ACT I

SCENE: *VATELIN's home in Paris. An elegant parlor. Door at rear. Door to bedrooms, R. Door to gallery and Vatelin's office, Left. Desk and Chair, L. Sofa and Chair, R. A pouf near the sofa. Fireplace at right.*

AT RISE: *The stage is empty for a moment. Before long we hear murmurs behind rear door, increasing in intensity until it becomes an uproar. LUCIENNE dressed for outside, and wearing a hat that's in disarray, comes in the door like a woman frightened out of her wits. She enters like a bomb, closes the door behind her, but not quickly enough to prevent a cane being thrust in the door by a man we cannot yet see. LUCIENNE cannot close the door, but she leans on it.*

LUCIENNE. Good God! Go away, monsieur. Go away at once.
PONTAGNAC. (*trying to open the door which LUCIENNE keeps pushing back*) Madame! Madame! Please, one moment!

LUCIENNE. Not on your life. What sort of a man are you? (*presses on door and calls*) Jean! Jean! Augustine! Oh, no one is here!

PONTAGNAC. Madame! Madame!

LUCIENNE. No! Go away!

PONTAGNAC. (*who has finally squeezed in*) I beg you to listen to me, madame.

LUCIENNE. You're disgraceful. I order you to leave this instant.

PONTAGNAC. Don't be frightened, Madame. You're in no danger. If my intentions are not altogether pure, I swear to you that they are not hostile. Quite the contrary. (*HE goes toward her.*)

LUCIENNE. (*retreating*) You're completely mad, monsieur.

PONTAGNAC. Yes, madame, you used the right word. I'm mad—mad for you. I know my conduct is audacious, and certainly not conventional, but I don't give a damn about that. I only know that I love you and that I had to use any means I could think of to get near you.

LUCIENNE. (*stopping to speak*) Monsieur, I won't listen to another word. Leave at once.

PONTAGNAC. Anything but that, madame—anything but that. I tell you I love you! (*new pursuit*) I had to see you! And now that I have, it's like a thunderbolt. I've been following you for eight days. You must have noticed me.

LUCIENNE. (*stopping in front of table*) No, monsieur.

PONTAGNAC. I'm sure you noticed me. A woman always notices a man who is following her.

LUCIENNE. What conceit!

PONTAGNAC. That's not conceit at all, merely observation.

LUCIENNE. I've had enough of this. I don't even know you.

PONTAGNAC. I don't know you either, madame, and that fact fills me with such remorse that I am going to do something about it immediately. Oh, madame—!

LUCIENNE. Monsieur!

PONTAGNAC. Oh, my dear Marguerite!

LUCIENNE. (*letting it slip out without realizing*) Lucienne!

PONTAGNAC. Thank you for telling me, Lucienne. What a lovely name.

LUCIENNE. Who gave you permission to use my first name? I forbid it!

PONTAGNAC. Don't try to tell me what I should call you.

LUCIENNE. What do you take me for? I'm a respectable woman.

PONTAGNAC. That's admirable. I adore respectable women.

LUCIENNE. Be careful, monsieur. I'm trying to avoid a scandal, but if you refuse to leave, I shall call my husband.

PONTAGNAC. Really now! Do you have a husband?

LUCIENNE. Of course I have.

PONTAGNAC. How cozy! But please—let us leave that imbecile out of this for a moment.

LUCIENNE. Are you calling my husband an imbecile?

PONTAGNAC. The husbands of women I like are always imbeciles.

LUCIENNE. (*going upstage*) Well, you'll see how that imbecile will deal with you. (*facing him defiantly*) So you don't want to leave?

PONTAGNAC. Less than ever.

LUCIENNE. (*calling to left*) Very well! Crépin!

PONTAGNAC. What a ridiculous name!
LUCIENNE. Crépin!
VATELIN. (*entering door left*) Did you call me, my dear?
PONTAGNAC. Oh! (*Recognizing VATELIN, he wants to crawl through the floor.*)
VATELIN. Pontagnac! My good friend.
LUCIENNE. What?
PONTAGNAC. Good old Vatelin.

(*THEY embrace warmly.*)

VATELIN. How have you been doing?
PONTAGNAC. Very well.

(*LUCIENNE looks on in a stupor, then goes down right, takes off her hat and puts it on sofa.*)

This is something of a surprise.
VATELIN. Why should it be a surprise? Since you are in my house isn't it natural to see me here?
PONTAGNAC. Huh? Oh—I meant—*I* am surprising *you*—that's what I meant.
VATELIN. Oh yes, of course.
LUCIENNE. (*to VATELIN*) Do you know this man?
VATELIN. Of course I know him.
PONTAGNAC. (*Ill at ease, HE loses his head.*) Yes—yes. (*takes some money from his pocket, sides up to LUCIENNE and says low*) Take this—take it—and not a word. (*puts the money in her hand*)
LUCIENNE. (*astonished, aside*) He's giving me money!
VATELIN. (*who saw none of the business*) Well, what's the matter with you?
PONTAGNAC. Me? Nothing. Why do you think

something is the matter?

VATELIN. You seemed restless, that's all. (*HE walks a little.*)

LUCIENNE. (*low to PONTAGNAC*) Take this back. What do you want me to do with it?

PONTAGNAC. I'm sorry—I lost my head. (*HE takes the money and quickly pockets it.*)

VATELIN. Ah, my good friend, you wouldn't believe how touched I am. I had almost given up hope of having you visit me, even though you have often promised to do so.

LUCIENNE. You mean that you just don't know how to thank monsieur.

VATELIN. (*while PONTAGNAC makes useless salutations that scarcely hide his confusion*) That's so. I must tell you it was kind of you to come, and especially like this—well—shall we say, on the spur of the moment?

LUCIENNE. Exactly! On the very prickly spur of the moment. (*SHE goes to fireplace.*)

PONTAGNAC. I'm delighted to be here, my friend—and madame. (*aside*) She's making a fool of me!

VATELIN. I was just realizing—you have never met my wife. My dear Lucienne, this is Monsieur Pontagnac, one of my good friends. Pontagnac—my wife, Lucienne.

PONTAGNAC. Madame—delighted.

VATELIN. Of course I don't know if I'm acting wisely in presenting Pontagnac to you.

PONTAGNAC. (*worried*) Why do you say that?

VATELIN. Because you're such a roving, rambunctious man-about-town. What a sinner! Do you mean that you didn't know your reputation? (*to LUCIENNE*) He can't see a woman without courting her. He wants them all.

LUCIENNE. (*laughing sarcastically*) All? That's not very

flattering to each one individually. (*turns to PONTAGNAC, sharply*) Is it?

PONTAGNAC. Oh, madame, your husband exaggerates. (*aside*) Why did the idiot have to say that?

LUCIENNE. (*by fireplace*) What a dreadful deception for the poor woman who believes she has been selected from among many, but ends up realizing she is just one girl in a regiment.

PONTAGNAC. I insist that I'm being misrepresented.

LUCIENNE. I must admit that I wouldn't be very proud to be a number in such an army. (*changing tone*) Won't you sit down? (*SHE sits in chair near fireplace.*)

PONTAGNAC. (*sitting on sofa, says aside*) She's laughing at me!

VATELIN. (*sitting near them*) My friend, I think my wife is putting you down.

PONTAGNAC. She's doing very well at it.

LUCIENNE. Some men must have a pitiful opinion of women, considering the way they treat us. Of course those who court us with charm, and with manners, at least show us a certain deference. But what about those who want to take us by assault, by following us in the street, for example?

PONTAGNAC. (*aside*) Here it comes!

VATELIN. (*laughing*) Following you in the street? Men who do that are thugs, or pimps, or brainless peasants.

LUCIENNE. (*very sweetly to PONTAGNAC*) Which suits you best?

PONTAGNAC. (*embarrassed*) Madame, I don't know why you say—

VATELIN. (*interrupting*) Oh, my wife was speaking in general terms.

LUCIENNE. Naturally.

PONTAGNAC. Of course. (*aside*) Some people shouldn't speak at all.

LUCIENNE. Well, I don't know your opinion, but it seems to me that if I were a man, I wouldn't enjoy that sort of conquest. One of two things would happen: the woman would reject me and I would be out in the cold again, or she would accept me warmly, and that would destroy any desire I had for the woman.

PONTAGNAC. Of course, of course. You must be right.

LUCIENNE. But that is not the opinion of all men — judging from those who insist on following *me*.

VATELIN. (*rises, goes to LUCIENNE*) Has someone been following you?

LUCIENNE. Constantly.

PONTAGNAC. Can't we talk of something else? This conversation is getting as one-sided as a judge's decree.

VATELIN. (*going to him*) Not at all — this interests me. After all, a man takes the liberty of following my wife in the street.

PONTAGNAC. But every so discreetly.

VATELIN. What do you know about it? A man who follows a woman is always indiscreet. (*directly to LUCIENNE*) Why didn't you mention this sooner?

LUCIENNE. What good would it do? I knew the man was just a weak, over-sexed moron, and not at all dangerous.

(*PONTAGNAC slaps his own cheek audibly.*)

VATELIN. But don't you think we should do something to rid you of this creature? It must be very annoying to have someone following on your heels.

LUCIENNE. Very boring, at least.

VATELIN. And it's humiliating for me. But there is surely something you could do. You could go into some shop for instance.

LUCIENNE. I did that. I went into a pastry shop, and he came in right behind me and bought a cream puff and two jelly-rolls.

VATELIN. A pastry shop is not the place to go when a man is following you. You should go into a jewelry shop. They wouldn't permit a loiterer. Why didn't you go into a jewelry shop?

LUCIENNE. I tried that, too. He was waiting for me at the door when I came out.

(*PONTAGNAC puts his head in both hands.*)

VATELIN. I can see that the man is as tenacious as a bulldog. (*to PONTAGNAC*) It's hard to believe that such ill-bred men live in our beautiful Paris.

PONTAGNAC. Yes – ill-bred. I agree – but can't we talk of something else?

VATELIN. It seems that a husband can't allow his wife to leave the house without subjecting her to the advances of some degenerate.

(*LUCIENNE gets up and sits on pouf.*)

PONTAGNAC. (*furious*) Vatelin!
VATELIN. What?
PONTAGNAC. You're going too far!
VATELIN. Never too far. I wish that demented creature would fall into my hands. (*a gesture of defiance*)

LUCIENNE. That wouldn't be difficult to arrange, would it, Monsieur Pontagnac?

PONTAGNAC. Oh, good heavens – what time is it?
VATELIN. Why – does he know the man?
LUCIENNE. Better than anyone. Why don't you tell us his name, Monsieur Pontagnac?
PONTAGNAC. (*on hot coals*) But, madame, do you really want – ?
LUCIENNE. Of course. His name is Pon – Pon – Pont-L'Evêque?
PONTAGNAC. That's possible – Pont-L'Evêque.
LUCIENNE. No! Pontagnac!
VATELIN. Pontagnac? You?
PONTAGNAC. (*with a very contrived laugh*) It was me – it was I – I was it. (*HE laughs crazily now.*) I'm the man.
VATELIN. (*laughing heartily*) Oh, what a joker.

(*LUCIENNE rises and goes to fireplace.*)

PONTAGNAC. But I knew with whom I was dealing. I knew that it was Madame Vatelin, and I said to myself: "I'm going to fashion a little intrigue. I'm going to pretend to be following her."
LUCIENNE. Pretend? That's good!
PONTAGNAC. I knew she would be surprised out of her shoes when we came face to face with her husband.
VATELIN. Oh, yes! Ta-ra-ta-ra! You didn't know a thing about it! Well, that will teach you to follow women in the street. You happen on the wife of a friend, and you find yourself way ahead of yourself. You've had a lesson.
PONTAGNAC. I own up to it. I confess. But you're not angry with me, are you?
VATELIN. Well, let's see about that. I know you're a friend – therefore – well – let me say that since I am very sure of my wife – the thing that bothers me in an adven-

ture of this sort is that it makes me appear like an idiot. A man follows my wife, and I say to myself: "He might know who she is." He meets me, and he thinks: "That's the woman's husband". So I look like an idiot. But you know that I know, and I know that you know that I know, and we both know that each of us knows what we know. So, it's a different matter. I don't feel that I look like an idiot.

PONTAGNAC. Of course not.

VATELIN. If anyone is bothered, I would say it's you.

PONTAGNAC. Me?

VATELIN. It always pains us to make a damn-fool blunder.

PONTAGNAC. In this case I don't agree, since it allowed me the pleasure of coming into your home.

VATELIN. I'm with you there. It was indeed a pleasure.

PONTAGNAC. You're too kind.

VATELIN. Not at all.

LUCIENNE. I'm really very happy to have been the bit of fluff that brought you two mighty male creatures together. (*SHE sits on sofa.*)

VATELIN. There's only one thing for you to do, Pontagnac, and that is to make your excuses to my wife.

PONTAGNAC. (*to LUCIENNE*) Oh, madame, you must find me very guilty. (*HE goes to fireplace*)

LUCIENNE. Oh, you bachelors are all the same.

VATELIN. Bachelor? Him? But he's married.

LUCIENNE. No!

VATELIN. Yes!

LUCIENNE. You're married? You?

PONTAGNAC. Yes—a little.

LUCIENNE. But that's horrible.

VATELIN. Do you think so?

LUCIENNE. It's frightful! How could he—?

PONTAGNAC. Oh, you know how it is—one fine day—you don't know how or why—you find yourself side by side with a woman—someone asks some questions—and you both say "I do," because there are so many people watching. But when the people have all gone away, you realize that you're married—and for life!

LUCIENNE. Oh, monsieur, you have no excuse.

PONTAGNAC. For being married? (*HE sinks into a chair.*)

LUCIENNE. No, for behaving as you do, even though you are married. What would Madame Pontagnac think of your conduct?

PONTAGNAC. I don't keep her informed on such matters.

LUCIENNE. Do you think that what you do is honest?

PONTAGNAC. Oh, oh.

LUCIENNE. Do you? You would think it dishonest to touch the least part of your wife's fortune, but when it's a question of other things that belong to her—her husband, her marital happiness, her social existence—you make short work of it. "Who wishes to share? Come on, come on, try it! There will always be enough left." Oh, you waste, you waste. What does it matter to you? It's your wife who pays. Do you consider that honest?

PONTAGNAC. Good God, if it's acknowledged that I can afford all the necessities of the household, then it seems to me—

LUCIENNE. Really? But it's a question of assets that don't belong to you. You have legally given them to your wife. You have no right to dispose of family jewels that do not belong to you alone.

PONTAGNAC. But permit me to say—I don't touch the capital—it's intact. I touch a little income from the capital, that's all. As long as I am keeping the largest part at home, you can't find fault if I make a few outside investments.

LUCIENNE. When you're married, you make no investments except as father of the family.

PONTAGNAC. You talk like a lawyer.

LUCIENNE. I would like to know what you would do if your wife were acting as you do – squandering on others what you believe is yours alone.

PONTAGNAC. That's a different matter.

LUCIENNE. Naturally. It's never the same thing for you men. You would deserve to have your wife throwing away community property here and there.

VATELIN. Be careful, Lucienne. Pontagnac is going to hate you if you demoralize him like that.

LUCIENNE. What I am saying is not really for him – it's for you – just in case you get the fanciful idea of following Monsieur Pontagnac's example.

VATELIN. Me? Oh!

LUCIENNE. You'd be ill-advised to follow in his footsteps, because with me, you wouldn't get far.

PONTAGNAC. True.

VATELIN. That sounds as if you find pleasure in the thought.

PONTAGNAC. Not at all – I said "true" just as one would say "it's not possible".

LUCIENNE. I don't know Madame Pontagnac but I feel sorry for her.

PONTAGNAC. Of course. I have never deceived my wife without feeling sorry for her.

LUCIENNE. You must be constantly feeling sorry for her.

VATELIN. At least, now that you know the way to our

ACT I   THE FRENCH HAVE A WORD   17

house, you should bring Madame Pontagnac. My wife and I would be very happy to meet her.

PONTAGNAC. I'm sure that she would be very happy too, but we can't think of it.

LUCIENNE. Why not?

PONTAGNAC. Because of her arthritis. She is completely bedridden because of it.

VATELIN. Really!

PONTAGNAC. She never leaves home – or, if she must leave, it's in a little wagon. We have a man who pulls it.

VATELIN. I'm sorry to hear that. I didn't know.

LUCIENNE. That's sad.

PONTAGNAC. You don't have to tell me.

VATELIN. It's a great pity. But we'll go to see her, if you will permit it.

PONTAGNAC. Of course. Why not?

VATELIN. Where does she live?

PONTAGNAC. At Pau – in the south of France.

VATELIN. Good God! That's a bit far.

PONTAGNAC. There's an express train. But what can I do? The region was recommended for her health.

VATELIN. Then she should stay there.

LUCIENNE. All the same, we regret it.

JEAN. (*entering*) Monsieur, there's an art dealer who has a landscape for you.

VATELIN. Oh, it's my Corot. I bought a Corot yesterday.

PONTAGNAC. Yes?

VATELIN. It was six hundred francs.

PONTAGNAC. That's very inexpensive. Is it signed?

(*LUCIENNE sits at right of desk.*)

VATELIN. It's signed all right—it's signed "Salevin". But the dealer says he guarantees the falseness of the signature.

PONTAGNAC. Who could resist that?

VATELIN. I simply take off the "Salevin" and nothing remains but the Corot. (*to JEAN*) I'll come in there. Have him take it into the gallery. Will you pardon me for a moment. I'll receive my painting, and I'll be back with you shortly. (*to PONTAGNAC*) I want you to see all my paintings. You know about such things and you can give me advice.

PONTAGNAC. I'll be glad to.

(*VATELIN goes out, left door.*)

LUCIENNE. Sit down.

PONTAGNAC. Do you mean that I don't frighten you any longer?

LUCIENNE. As you can see.

PONTAGNAC. (*sitting*) I must have appeared very ridiculous to you.

LUCIENNE. (*smiling*) Do you think so? Well, you're right.

PONTAGNAC. You're a scoffer!

LUCIENNE. Tell me—what you possibly could have hoped for by following me, and with such desperate eagerness.

PONTAGNAC. What any healthy man of my age would hope for when he follows a woman he doesn't know.

LUCIENNE. You're nothing if not candid.

PONTAGNAC. Well now, if I told you that I was following you in order to ask you what your thoughts were on Voltaire, you probably wouldn't have believed me.

LUCIENNE. You amuse me. Do your little capers always succeed? I mean, are there women who – uh – uh – ?

PONTAGNAC. Yes, there are women who – uh – uh. Shall we say thirty-three and one third percent?

LUCIENNE. You had bad luck today. You stumbled on one of the sixty-six and two thirds. (*SHE rises.*)

PONTAGNAC. (*rises and puts down hat and cane*) Oh, madame, don't speak of that. If you only knew how sorry I am.

LUCIENNE. You should be.

PONTAGNAC. What can I do? It's a misfortune to have a temperment like mine, but it's stronger than I am. I have women in my blood.

LUCIENNE. But legally you're entitled to only one.

PONTAGNAC. My wife, of course. She's a charming woman. But she's always been that for me. It's a love story that I have re-read many times.

LUCIENNE. But of course now it is perhaps not so easy to turn the pages.

PONTAGNAC. Why so?

LUCIENNE. Because of her arthritis, I mean.

PONTAGNAC. My wife? Since when?

LUCIENNE. But you're the one who told us that –

PONTAGNAC. (*quickly regaining his senses*) Oh, yes, yes, yes – my wife – in Pau, in the south of France.

LUCIENNE. Yes, that's what you said.

PONTAGNAC. And yet you tell me I have no excuse. Come, now! When heaven puts a divine, exquisite creature within my sight, I –

LUCIENNE. (*as PONTAGNAC comes towards desk, she crosses R, sits in chair R of sofa*) Enough of that chapter, monsieur. I think you have made honest amends.

PONTAGNAC. Admit to me – frankly – you're in love with

someone else.

LUCIENNE. Do you know that you can be the most exasperating of men?

PONTAGNAC. Why do you say that?

LUCIENNE. You won't admit that a woman can be a faithful wife. If she resists you, it's because she loves someone else. There can be no other motivation. What women are you in the habit of associating with?

PONTAGNAC. That's a very long story. But I'd like to tell you something if you promise not to confide it to anyone.

LUCIENNE. (*sitting in chair*) Not even to my husband.

PONTAGNAC. (*sitting on pouf*) That's all I ask. Well, I have great difficulty in believing that you can love your husband. (*HE edges the pouf nearer to LUCIENNE.*)

LUCIENNE. What an idea! Please, back away!

(*HE comes closer with pouf.*)

Back away!

PONTAGNAC. Pardon me, I wasn't thinking. Certainly he's a fine fellow and I'm fond of him.

LUCIENNE. I can see that.

PONTAGNAC. But, confidentially, he doesn't appear to be a man who would inspire great passion.

LUCIENNE. (*severely*) He's my husband!

PONTAGNAC. (*rising*) You see! You agree with me.

LUCIENNE. Not at all!

PONTAGNAC. Oh, yes. If you loved him – I mean real love and not mere affection – would you have to qualify your love? A woman who really loves, says "I love him because I love", she doesn't say, "I love him because he's my husband". Love is not a by-product, it's the principal merchandise. It only exists, and it is only worth having, in the pure state of an essence. But you've been using eau de Cologne.

LUCIENNE. You talk like a perfumer.

PONTAGNAC. Tell me what the husband proves. Any man can be a husband. All he needs to do is pass the board of examiners. He needs no more qualification than would be required for a job at the complaint desk of a department store. (*sits on pouf again*) But the lover! That's another matter. He must have spirit, he must have flame. He is the artist of love. The husband is only a plumber's helper.

LUCIENNE. I see. Then it's as an artist of love that you came—?

PONTAGNAC. Exactly right.

LUCIENNE. Well, monsieur, perhaps I'm going to appear ridiculous to you, but I have the good fortune to be married to a man who is both a plumber's helper and what you call an artist of love.

PONTAGNAC. That's a rare bird.

LUCIENNE. I desire nothing more as long as he doesn't peddle his artistic qualities outside of this house.

PONTAGNAC. Oh, really? And if he did go outside the house?

LUCIENNE. (*rising*) That would be another matter. In that case I would go to extremes.

PONTAGNAC. (*rises*) That's good of you.

LUCIENNE. But there is no question of that now. I would never be the first to have an affair—only the second—and quickly, just as I was saying the other day to my cousin.

PONTAGNAC. (*incredulous*) Your cousin?

LUCIENNE. One of my cousins who insisted on knowing if I would decide to roam someday.

JEAN. (*coming in to announce*) Monsieur Rédillon is here.

(*REDILLON comes in behind him, without ceremony.*)

LUCIENNE. Come in, my dear friend – and come to my aid in order to edify this gentleman here. (*introducing*) Monsieur Ernest Rédillon, Monsieur Pontagnac. You are both friends of my husband. (*THEY shake hands.*) Tell this gentleman that you know very well that I am a model wife, and would never deceive my husband unless I had just cause.

REDILLON. Why a question like that?

LUCIENNE. Please, tell him. He wants to know.

REDILLON. (*squirming*) This gentleman? You two must have been having a charming conversation. The devil take me if I didn't intrude at exactly the wrong time.

LUCIENNE. Of course not. Didn't I call you to my aid?

PONTAGNAC. Oh, we were just teasing each other.

REDILLON. Oh, that's it. Monsieur is undoubtedly an old friend, an intimate friend, although I don't recall ever having seen him here before.

LUCIENNE. I've known him for just twenty minutes.

REDILLON. This is getting better and better. Well, my dear Lucienne, I regret that I won't be able to answer the question that you have put to me. I have too much respect for women to engage in conversation that would be out of place. I declare myself incompetent.

PONTAGNAC. I think I'm being given a lesson.

REDILLON. Isn't Vatelin here?

LUCIENNE. Yes, he's here. He's having a tête-à-tête with a Corot. I'll go see if he got lost in the landscape,

ACT I   THE FRENCH HAVE A WORD   23

and I'll bring him back to you. You two know each other now, so talk about me while I'm gone. (*SHE goes out L. There is a moment of silence as the two men look each other over, always on the sly.*)

PONTAGNAC. (*aside*) This must be the cousin she meant.

(*There is a silent scene as the two men look at things in the room, paintings, books and so forth, one on right, one on left. They come down little by little. They try to steal a look at each other but affect an indifferent air when their glances happen to meet. REDILLON gains the sofa and sits, then starts a monotonous whistle.*)

PONTAGNAC. (*seated near desk*) I beg pardon?
REDILLON. Monsieur?
PONTAGNAC. I thought you were speaking to me.
REDILLON. No, I wasn't.
PONTAGNAC. Excuse me.
REDILLON. No harm done.

(*Begins whistling again, and PONTAGNAC, irritated, begins humming loudly. REDILLON takes a newspaper from his pocket, unfolds it and turns his back on PONTAGNAC to read. PONTAGNAC picks up a magazine and thumbs through it nervously.*)

LUCIENNE. (*entering*) I hate to interrupt this interesting conversation.

(*REDILLON closes his newspaper, PONTAGNAC his book.*)

My husband is eager to show you his Corot, Monsieur Pontagnac.

PONTAGNAC. He is?

LUCIENNE. Take the door there, and then straight ahead.

PONTAGNAC. (*without enthusiasm*) This way?

LUCIENNE. Yes. Hurry, now.

PONTAGNAC. (*taking hat and cane from table*) Yes, of course. (*turns to REDILLON*) Perhaps monsieur would like to come also?

REDILLON. Me?

LUCIENNE. No, he is not interested in art.

PONTAGNAC. Very well, then. (*HE goes out door left, giving a look at the two.*)

LUCIENNE. Sit down, my dear friend.

REDILLON. (*who has been nervously walking back and forth*) Thank you. I was walking because I needed a little exercise.

LUCIENNE. (*to fireplace*) What's the matter with you?

REDILLON. Nothing. Do I look as if something is wrong?

LUCIENNE. Yes. You look like a bear in a cage. Was it the presence of Monsieur Pontagnac that ruffled you?

REDILLON. What do I care about him? He's nothing to me.

LUCIENNE. I thought perhaps—

REDILLON. He doesn't worry me in the least. (*after a pause*) Who is that character anyway?

LUCIENNE. I thought you weren't bothered about him.

REDILLON. Pardon me if I'm indiscreet.

LUCIENNE. You're pardoned.

REDILLON. You're so good. (*after a moment*) Was he

trying to make love to you?
LUCIENNE. Yes.
REDILLON. Oh, that's disgusting!
LUCIENNE. Do you have an exclusive permit?
REDILLON. That's not the same thing. I love you.
LUCIENNE. He said that he did too.
REDILLON. That's terrible. A man you've known only ten minutes.
LUCIENNE. Twenty!
REDILLON. Ten or twenty! I wasn't holding a clock on you.
LUCIENNE. Actually, I was introduced to him only twenty minutes ago, but I've known him by sight for eight days while he was following me in the street.
REDILLON. I can't believe it!
LUCIENNE. It's true.
REDILLON. He's a low, uncouth rotter.
LUCIENNE. (*by fireplace*) Thank you – for him.
REDILLON. So your husband thought it was clever to introduce him to you.

(*LUCIENNE smiles and extends arms in gesture of confirmation.*)

Oh, these husbands. I think they purposely create dangers for themselves.
LUCIENNE. But, Rédillon.
REDILLON. I say what I think. And when the danger comes – as it usually does – they complain. Why does Vatelin have to introduce men into his household? Do we need them? Shouldn't our little threesome be enough for him? (*seeing LUCIENNE laugh*) It's true. I can't bear to see a man near you. It makes me furious. (*a knee on*

pouf) But I can't tell your husband that.

LUCIENNE. (*going to him*) Calm down, Casanova.

REDILLON. (*almost crying*) I knew that something dreadful would happen today. (*HE walks downstage.*)

LUCIENNE. Why?

REDILLON. Because I dreamed that my teeth were falling out. All forty-five of them! And when I dream that my teeth fall out, it never fails. The last time, someone stole my little dog that I was very attached to. Today they are trying to steal my mistress.

LUCIENNE. Your mistress! Now wait a moment! I am not your mistress.

REDILLON. You're mistress of my heart, and nobody can prevent that—not even you.

LUCIENNE. Until you release me from my responsibility.

REDILLON. Oh, swear to me that you will never love that man.

LUCIENNE. That man? But you're foolish, my friend. Is he the only man I know? Do you think I pay any attention to him?

REDILLON. Oh, thank you. Did you notice how disagreeable looking he is? And did you notice his nose? With a nose like that, a man is incapable of love.

LUCIENNE. Oh!

REDILLON. But look at my nose. I have a nose made for love, an amorous nose, a loving nose, a captivating, bewitching, seductive nose.

LUCIENNE. How do you know all that?

REDILLON. I've been told.

LUCIENNE. I see.

REDILLON. Lucienne, don't forget that you promised you would never belong to anyone but me.

ACT I   THE FRENCH HAVE A WORD   27

LUCIENNE. Correction. *If* I ever belong to anyone at all. But for that, my dear friend, a certain combination of circumstances is necessary. (*SHE sits R. of desk.*)

REDILLON. Yes, I know. It depends on whether your husband deceives you. I wish he would hurry. What is he waiting for?

(*LUCIENNE gives him a gesture of reproach.*)

Don't you feel the cruelty of the torture you impose on me? I'm like a diner to whom they keep serving appetizers, but never bring the main dish.

LUCIENNE. Poor boy! You must be stuffed with hors d'oeuvres. You'll have to dine somewhere else.

REDILLON. I do! What do you expect? I'm made of flesh and bones and blood. And sometimes I get hungry. I'm hungry now, I tell you, I'm hungry.

LUCIENNE. Stop that! You're ugly when you start crying famine.

REDILLON. You laugh at me – heartlessly. (*HE sits on pouf.*)

LUCIENNE. Or do you think we should both cry, now that I know you partake of some extra sustenance?

REDILLON. Extra! You can have all my extras. Would I have any extras if you were willing? But you're not willing, so what can I do? I realize it's not fair to you, but the extras derive some benefit from it.

LUCIENNE. (*Her back to the desk*) I hope they enjoy it.

REDILLON. I can speak for them – they do.

LUCIENNE. And this is the man who comes to speak to me of his great love.

REDILLON. Absolutely. What's to prevent it? It's not my fault if there exists both love and the – the –

LUCIENNE. The what?
REDILLON. The animal.
LUCIENNE. That's true. But can't you bring yourself to kill the animal?
REDILLON. I was taught never to be cruel to dumb beasts.
LUCIENNE. Poor pussycat. Perhaps you could lead it on a leash.
REDILLON. That's what I do, but the animal is stronger than I am. It leads, and I follow. What do you want of me? When I can't do otherwise, I give in. (*HE gains the right.*) I take a walk with the animal.
LUCIENNE. Oh, men! Poor Ernest! What is her name? (*SHE is on sofa.*)
REDILLON. Who?
LUCIENNE. Your walk? Your animal?
REDILLON. Pluplu. That's short for Pluchette.
LUCIENNE. Delightful!
REDILLON. (*going to her*) But the heart has nothing to do with it, you know. Pluplu doesn't really count. There is only one woman in my eyes, and that is you. What does it matter which altar I sacrifice on, if it's to you that I say my prayers?
LUCIENNE. That's very sweet.
REDILLON. It's true. My body is near Pluplu, but my thoughts are for you. When I'm with her, I try to imagine that it's you. She's in my arms, but it's you I think I'm holding. I tell her to keep quiet so that I won't hear her voice. I close my eyes and I say: "Oh, Lucienne, oh Lucienne."
LUCIENNE. But that's encroachment. I don't like it! Does she accept it?
REDILLON. Pluplu? Very well. She even feels obliged

to do the same as I. She closes her eyes and says: "Oh, Pierre, oh, Pierre."

LUCIENNE. (*rising and walking*) Oh, that's wonderful. You could say it's an act done by understudies.

REDILLON. (*intensely*) Oh, Lucienne, Lucienne, when will you put an end to the torture I endure? When will you say to me: "Redillon, I am yours – do with me as you like."

LUCIENNE. But do you–?

REDILLON. (*on his knees before her*) Lucienne, I love you.

LUCIENNE. Will you get up! My husband might come in. He's already surprised you three times before, on your knees like this.

REDILLON. It makes no difference to me. Let him come in. Let him see me.

LUCIENNE. Not at all. I won't have it. Such an idea!

(*SHE pushes him to make him rise, but the force makes him fall back, seated on the floor. LUCIENNE disengages herself and goes to sit at table.*)

REDILLON. As I was saying, dear Lucienne.

VATELIN. (*enter L, sees REDILLON on the floor*) Well, well – there you are – on the floor again.

REDILLON. As you can see. How goes it?

VATELIN. Not badly, thank you. (*to PONTAGNAC who came in behind him*) He has a mania for sitting on the floor. This is my friend Rédillon. Monsieur Rédillon, Monsieur Pontagnac.

PONTAGNAC. We've already met.

VATELIN. Oh! I've never seen anything like this. Every

time he waits for me to come in here—and the room is not lacking in chairs—I find him with his behind on the floor.

PONTAGNAC. (*dryly*) Oh.

REDILLON. It's a childhood habit. I used to love to roll on the carpet. Well, every time I go anywhere, I find myself preferring to sit on the floor than a chair.

VATELIN. Strange habit. Maybe your mother was frightened by the man who delivered the carpets.

REDILLON. (*getting up*) Very funny!

PONTAGNAC. (*aside*) What a stupid husband!

LUCIENNE. Well, have you seen my husband's paintings?

VATELIN. I should say he has. He was amazed. He said the museums don't have paintings like that. Didn't you, my friend?

PONTAGNAC. Quite right. You wouldn't find them in any museum. (*aside*) They're all fakes!

(*The doorbell rings.*)

VATELIN. It's too bad that your wife is in such a state. I would be proud to show her my gallery.

PONTAGNAC. But with her arthritis, she's in Pau—in the south of France—you know.

VATELIN. Oh, yes, in the little wagon. I remember. I pity humans who suffer so.

ALL. (*with a sigh*) Oh, yes!

JEAN. (*enters, announcing*) Madame Pontagnac.

ALL. Huh!

PONTAGNAC. It's my wife!

ALL. Your wife!

LUCIENNE. I thought she was in Pau.

ACT I   THE FRENCH HAVE A WORD   31

VATELIN. Yes, with her arthritis.
PONTAGNAC. She must have been cured. It's a remarkable climate down there. (*to JEAN*) We're not in. Tell her we're not in.
LUCIENNE. But we'd love to see her. Have her come in.
PONTAGNAC. That's what I said. Have her come in. (*aside*) Oh, la, la! (*aloud*) My friends, for reasons that I will explain later, don't say a word if my wife questions you. Just follow my lead.
MADAME PONTAGNAC. (*enters*) I beg your pardon, Messieurs, madame.
PONTAGNAC. Oh, my darling, here you are. What a wonderful surprise. I was just leaving. We'll go together. Say good-bye to these delightful people and we'll be on our way.
MADAME PONTAGNAC. But I'm not ready to leave. I just got here.
PONTAGNAC. Of course you are ready to go.
MADAME PONTAGNAC. I am not!
LUCIENNE. Stay awhile, Madame. Your husband can leave if he must.
MADAME PONTAGNAC. (*sitting on chair which VATELIN offers. REDILLON sits at desk.*) Excuse me, Madame, for coming here without knowing you.
LUCIENNE. But Madame, I am delighted that you came.
VATELIN. (*one knee on pouf*) Certainly — believe us.
MADAME PONTAGNAC. I've heard my husband speak of you for so long.
VATELIN. Really? That was good of him.
MADAME PONTAGNAC. So I said to myself that this state of affairs can't continue — the husbands are intimate friends, but the wives don't even know each other.
LUCIENNE AND VATELIN. Very intimate.

MADAME PONTAGNAC. You can really say that my husband loves you. I was almost jealous. Every day the same thing: "Where are you going?" "To the Vatelins." Always the Vatelins.

PONTAGNAC. (*quickly*) You haven't seen the gallery, have you? Come to see his paintings. They're worth the trouble.

MADAME PONTAGNAC. Not now! What's wrong with you?

PONTAGNAC. Nothing is wrong with me.

VATELIN. What does all this mean?

REDILLON. (*aside*) This is fun, this is fun.

MADAME PONTAGNAC. You seem agitated. Are you?

PONTAGNAC. Me? Agitated? Why should I be agitated? But why do you waste time telling the Vatelins that I come here every day? They already know that very well.

LUCIENNE. Oh! (*exchanges look with VATELIN*)

VATELIN. I understand.

PONTAGNAC. (*making signs to VATELIN*) You know that I come here every day, don't you Vatelin?

VATELIN. Yes, yes, yes, yes.

PONTAGNAC. There—you see.

REDILLON. (*doing his own little rescue work*) I've met him here quite often.

PONTAGNAC. (*low to REDILLON*) Huh? Thanks.

REDILLON. (*low*) Don't mention it.

PONTAGNAC. Well, are you convinced?

MADAME PONTAGNAC. Perfectly. (*getting up, goes L*)

VATELIN. (*to PONTAGNAC, low*) I'll get you out of this. (*to MADAME PONTAGNAC*) Believe me, madame, your dear husband speaks of you quite often—during his frequent visits.

MADAME PONTAGNAC. Really?

VATELIN. I would have asked him to introduce me to you some time ago if I hadn't known you were in Pau.

MADAME PONTAGNAC. Pau?

PONTAGNAC. (*aside*) Another avalanche! (*aloud, as he swings VATELIN around to put him between him and his wife*) No! No! Who says "Pau"? You must have said "oh", or "no", or "Jo". Where are you taking Jo?

VATELIN. What? Where am I taking–?

PONTAGNAC. Yes. Who said anything about Pau?

VATELIN. (*trying to save the situation*) Not Pau! I was saying "so". *So*, if I had known you were–you were–

PONTAGNAC. Nowhere!

VATELIN. (*not knowing what he is saying*) That's right! If I had known that you were nowhere.

PONTAGNAC. (*low to VATELIN*) Oh, shut up!

VATELIN. (*low to PONTAGNAC*) I'd like to, because I don't know what I'm saying.

REDILLON. (*aside*) People babble around here.

MADAME PONTAGNAC. Oh, Monsieur Vatelin, you don't have to make excuses. I knew that I could not count on a visit from you, because my husband informed me of your condition.

PONTAGNAC. (*aside*) Another bomb!

VATELIN. My condition?

MADAME PONTAGNAC. Yes. You are suffering from arthritis.

VATELIN. No! It's you.

MADAME PONTAGNAC. Not I–you. Don't you have to be pulled in a little wagon when you go out?

VATELIN. I beg your pardon, but it's you.

PONTAGNAC. (*rushing to VATELIN*) Of course it's you. Don't try to hide it. You don't have to be coy in front of my wife. You're among friends.

VATELIN. Oh, yes, I also have to be pulled in a wagon.
PONTAGNAC. No! Not "also". Just you. You alone. (*drags VATELIN to left*) Let me see the rest of your paintings. You must have some more. I want to see them all.
VATELIN. I'll show you. Let's go to my gallery.
MADAME PONTAGNAC. Edmond, do you want to stay?

(*LUCIENNE rises.*)

PONTAGNAC. I'll be back, I'll be back.
VATELIN. Yes, we'll be back.

(*THEY leave at left.*)

MADAME PONTAGNAC. I've had all I can stand. Madame Vatelin, be very frank with me. Are certain people making fun of me?
LUCIENNE. I'm afraid so, Madame.

(*MADAME PONTAGNAC sits on chair near pouf.*)

Considering the way men always take up for each other, I think there should be a little solidarity among women. Yes, they were making a fool of you. (*SHE sits.*)
MADAME PONTAGNAC. I strongly suspected it.
LUCIENNE. Your husband is not an intimate friend of my husband. He knows my husband, yes, but he has never set foot in this house until today.
MADAME PONTAGNAC. I can't believe it.
LUCIENNE. You must always believe the worst about a man. If you found him here today, it wasn't because he came to see an old friend, but because he pursued a woman to this very room.

MADAME PONTAGNAC. A woman?
LUCIENNE. Yes. You're looking at the woman.
MADAME PONTAGNAC. Oh, no!
LUCIENNE. (*imitating her surprise*) Oh, yes! After having followed me down the street insisting that I had all the qualifications—of a—
REDILLON. (*peacefully in his chair at the desk*) A horizontal?
LUCIENNE. Yes.
MADAME PONTAGNAC. The cheat!
LUCIENNE. He was very disappointed to find that the woman was the wife of one of his friends. It was not his lucky day. But you can be sure your husband has lied to you. All his pretended visits here were simply a cover for his escapades.
MADAME PONTAGNAC. The miserable wretch!
REDILLON. A perfect description.
LUCIENNE. (*rising*) Excuse me for speaking to you so brutally, but you asked for frankness, and I've been nothing if not frank.
MADAME PONTAGNAC. You did what is right, and I thank you for it.
LUCIENNE. I only hope that someone is as frank with me if my husband ever decides to—
REDILLON. It's no use. With him, there is nothing going on. He's not interested.
LUCIENNE. I'm happy for that.
MADAME PONTAGNAC. I've had my suspicions for some time, and now I know I wasn't mistaken. (*pacing, looking towards direction her husband went*) It's between us, dear Pontagnac. I'll play the dummy, I'll spy on you, I'll keep you on the run, I'll surprise you in the act, and then—
LUCIENNE. And then?

MADAME PONTAGNAC. (*taking chair and putting it near sofa*) That's all I can say.
LUCIENNE. The law of retaliation?
MADAME PONTAGNAC. All the way!
LUCIENNE. An eye for an eye!
MADAME PONTAGNAC. Both eyes!
LUCIENNE. Bravo! It's the law of the jungle—the law of the new women's solidarity group. (*SHE embraces MADAME PONTAGNAC.*) The same goes for me. If my husband ever—
REDILLON. Hurrah!
MADAME PONTAGNAC. After all, I'm young, and I'm pretty.
LUCIENNE. So am I.
MADAME PONTAGNAC. Perhaps I didn't sound very modest.
REDILLON. To hell with that! When a woman is angry she doesn't have to be modest.
MADAME PONTAGNAC. In any case, I'm sure I can find some idiotic man who would be delighted to—
REDILLON. (*raising hand*) Present!
LUCIENNE. So could I. That's true, isn't it Redillon?
REDILLON. You? Oh, la la!
MADAME PONTAGNAC. And don't think that I will waste time looking for him. That would prevent me from savoring my vengeance. I'll take the first imbecile that comes along.
REDILLON. (*raising his hand*) Present!
MADAME PONTAGNAC. (*to REDILLON*) It can be you, if that would give you pleasure.
REDILLON. I? Oh, Madame.
LUCIENNE. Absolutely. And he's mine too if the need arises.

REDILLON. Oh, Lucienne. (*rises and goes to her*)
MADAME PONTAGNAC. Give me your name and address.
REDILLON. Ernest Rédillon, 17 Rue Caumartin.
MADAME PONTAGNAC. Redillon, 17 Rue Caumartin. Good! Well, monsieur, the moment is very near. When I surprise my husband in the act, I'll run to you and say "take me, I'm yours." (*SHE lets herself fall into his arms.*)
LUCIENNE. So will I, Rédillon. I'm yours. (*SHE also falls into his arms.*)
REDILLON. (*holding up both women*) Oh, ladies, it's astounding how lucky I am when there are strings tied to it.

(*Noises of voices. The three quickly separate and change positions.*)

MADAME PONTAGNAC. Our husbands are coming. Not a word. (*to VATELIN and her husband who stand by the door*) Come in, gentlemen. Why do you stand by the door?
VATELIN. No reason. Nothing at all.
MADAME PONTAGNAC. Have you seen all the paintings? Are you satisfied?
PONTAGNAC. Delighted. He has some exceptional canvases – done by relatives of the great masters.
VATELIN. That's right.
PONTAGNAC. He has one by Corot's son, one by Toulouse-Lautrec's second cousin, and one by Fragonard's sister-in-law. Really, there's no need to have the masters themselves.
VATELIN. That's what I always say. Sometimes they are even more carefully done than paintings by the masters.
REDILLON. And they cost a lot less.
MADAME PONTAGNAC. While you were admiring the

paintings, Madame Vatelin and I have become better acquainted. We talked about you a great deal.

PONTAGNAC. Oh?

MADAME PONTAGNAC. And monsieur said he had met you and that he admired you very much.

PONTAGNAC. He said that? (*to REDILLON*) I don't believe I introduced my wife. Monsieur Rédillon, Madame Pontagnac.

MADAME PONTAGNAC. Oh, we've had time to get well acquainted. (*SHE joins LUCIENNE above table.*)

PONTAGNAC. That's excellent. (*to REDILLON*) My wife receives on Fridays, if you care to give us the honor.

REDILLON. Why not?

JEAN. (*entering*) There is a lady who asks for Monsieur Vatelin.

VATELIN. Who is it?

JEAN. I don't know. It's the first time I've seen her. She talks funny, but she's a lady.

LUCIENNE. A lady? What does she want?

VATELIN. You should have asked her name.

LUCIENNE. (*to JEAN*) Is she pretty?

(*JEAN makes a grimace that doesn't say much.*)

VATELIN. What is that supposed to mean, Jean? (*to LUCIENNE*) Please, my dear, it's not up to the servants to give opinions on our visitors. (*to JEAN*) Did you say I was in?

JEAN. Yes, the lady is waiting for you in the small parlor.

VATELIN. That's good. Have her wait. I'll receive her.

(*JEAN goes out.*)

MADAME PONTAGNAC. Well, Monsieur Vatelin, I see that you will be busy, and I don't want to hinder you, especially when you have a lady to receive.

VATELIN. Oh, it's some client. There's no hurry. It's not the man she comes to see, but the lawyer.

LUCIENNE. I hope you're right.

MADAME PONTAGNAC. Good-bye, dear madame, and Monsieur – uh –

PONTAGNAC. Rédillon.

REDILLON. 17 Rue Caumartin.

MADAME PONTAGNAC. (*to her husband*) Make a note of that.

REDILLON. I'll go down with you. I have some errands to run. (*to LUCIENNE*) Au revoir, Madame. (*low*) Au revoir, my darling Lucienne. (*to VATELIN*) Au revoir, you!

PONTAGNAC. Let's go. (*HE shakes hands with VATELIN, then LUCIENNE, then low to them.*) As soon as I take my wife home, I'll come back and explain my actions.

MADAME PONTAGNAC. Are you coming?

PONTAGNAC. I'm coming.

(*THEY go out.*)

VATELIN. My dear, why don't you leave me alone so I can take care of this person?

LUCIENNE. I'll see you later, Crépin. (*SHE leaves, right, taking her hat which was on sofa.*)

(*VATELIN rings and JEAN enters.*)

VATELIN. Have the lady come in.

(*JEAN ushers in MARIA, then retires.*)

VATELIN. (*seated at desk, arranging papers, and without even looking at the person entering*) Will you please sit down, Madame?

(*MARIA comes behind him and gives him two big kisses on the eyes. SHE has a pronounced Spanish accent, and she is a whirlwind of Latin energy.*)

MARIA. Oh, mi amor! Mi cariño!
VATELIN. (*astonished, rises*) Who is it? What do you want? (*recognizing MARIA*) Oh, it's you, Madame Soldignac. Maria!
MARIA. Sí, it is the same one, amorcito.
VATELIN. But what are you doing here? This is madness.
MARIA. Why you say?
VATELIN. What about Madrid?
MARIA. Madrid is steel there, en España. But I leev Madrid. Can you no see that?
VATELIN. But what about your husband?
MARIA. I breeng heem. He come for beez-ness in Parees.
VATELIN. (*falling back in his chair*) But why have you come? What have you come to do here?
MARIA. What I come to do? Oh, you are bad hombre. How can you say thees ting? What I come to do? I geev up eber-ting for you. I am bad wife because of you.
VATELIN. Yes, yes. (*HE goes to listen at his wife's door.*)
MARIA. Salí de Madrid, cruzo el mar para verle, y cuando finalmente lo encuentro, me dijo, "por qué vienes aquí?"
VATELIN. I don't understand a word you're saying. Tell

me so I can understand. Why are you here? What do you want?

MARIA. What I want? You ask Maria what she want? She want choo.

VATELIN. Me?

MARIA. (*SHE goes behind desk.*) Chess! I luv you! Jess for you I leave Madrid, I cross in a ship and I get very seeck. I get sea-seeck. Oh, so sea-seeck! And I—(*leans over desk, gesturing vomiting*)

VATELIN. I understand. But what now?

MARIA. I am here for seben days. I come to see you. We make luv for seben days. Qué dices, mi amor?

VATELIN. (*collapsing in chair*) You'll be here a week?

MARIA. One week for you, querido mío. Oh, tell me you luv me steel. (*Suddenly SHE slams her hand on the desk.*) Why you no answer my letters? I say to me, Cray-peen no luv me no more. Oh, Cray-peen, tell me you luv me.

VATELIN. Yes, yes, of course.

MARIA. When I come to Pa-rees thees morning, I write letter to you, but I throw it in wastebasket. I say to me, Cray-peen no answer. So I take a cab. Oh, it is muy difícil. The man no understand me when I say Boo-lay-var Chop-el-lay.

VATELIN. (*correcting her*) Boulevard Chapelle. (*sadly*) But you found me.

MARIA. Yes, Cray-peen, and I am so happy. You come to see me tonight, no?

VATELIN. If possible, if possible.

MARIA. Doan tell me no. I find very nice little room—like I tell you in letter I throw in waste basket—forty-eight Roo Rock-ay-peen-ay.

VATELIN. Do you mean the Rue Roquépine? Are you

staying in the Rue Roquépine?

MARIA. No, I am weeth my husband in hotel on Campos eliseos, but the little room is for us. You come tonight?

VATELIN. No!

MARIA. Why you say "no"?

VATELIN. Because it's impossible. I'm not free. I have a wife. I'm a married man.

MARIA. You got wife?

VATELIN. I certainly have.

MARIA. But in Madrid you tell me you are willower.

VATELIN. What? Willower?

MARIA. You say your wife dead and you willower.

VATELIN. Widower! That was a figure of speech. I had left my wife in Paris so I was temporarily a widower.

MARIA. So what now? Everting feeneesh?

VATELIN. Maria, just be reasonable.

MARIA. You doan luv me no more? Not never?

VATELIN. Yes – when I come to Madrid.

MARIA. (*Crying loudly, SHE sits in chair.*) Oh, Cray-peen no luv me no more. Cray-peen no luv me.

VATELIN. Quiet! My wife might hear you.

MARIA. Es igual! I doan care.

VATELIN. But I care. Let's talk about this. Naturally I'm deeply touched, but I didn't expect the little affair that began in Madrid to become eternal. I met you and your husband on the boat from Marseille. We were all seasick. In Madrid you came to see me at my hotel every day. Please, let us be content to recall those days without starting them over again. In Madrid, I had an excuse. My wife was many miles away. There was an ocean between us. But here I have no excuse. Do as I do – make a sacrifice. Forget me. There are other men in Paris.

MARIA. No, I cannot. I am faithful woman. I wan only

ACT I   THE FRENCH HAVE A WORD   43

one lover and that is my Cray-peen. (*SHE rises, crosses to VATELIN.*)
    VATELIN. Yes, you're faithful to a certain point. But what about your husband?
    MARIA. I never have only one husband.
    VATELIN. That's very exemplary.
    MARIA. One husband. One lover. Bastante!
    VATELIN. So that's your principle?
    MARIA. Cray-peen, you doan wan me no more?
    VATELIN. Please realize—
    MARIA. Muy bien! Adios, Cray-peen.
    VATELIN. (*goes to door at rear*) Adios, dear señora—this way.
    MARIA. (*sitting in chair*) Doan poosh me out! I was suspeesh when you doan answer my letters. I wrote letter to my husband. Now I will send it to him.
    VATELIN. What does it say?
    MARIA. I read eet to you. (*SHE reads, rapidly.*) "Adios querido mío, olvidame. No soy mas que una esposa culpable y no me queda mas que morir. He sido la querida de Señor Vatelin, veinte-ocho Boulevard Chapelle quién me dió calabazas y ahora me voy a matar."
    VATELIN. That's beautiful. Send it! What does it mean?
    MARIA. You doan understand nuttin. (*translating as she looks at letter*) Good-bye dear, forget me. I am unfaithful wife who has nothing left but to die.
    VATELIN. What?
    MARIA. (*translating*) I have been mistress of Monsieur Vatelin, 28 Boulevard Chop-pel-lay.
    VATELIN. What? You put my name and address in it?
    MARIA. (*translating*) He has jeelted me and now I suicide myself.
    VATELIN. That's crazy! You can't send that, and you

can't commit suicide.

MARIA. I no commit it—I really *do* it. I shoot bullet inside my head.

VATELIN. Never! You can't kill yourself. Not with my name and address in the letter.

MARIA. Yes, your address—veinte-ocho bou-lay-var Chop-pel-lay.

VATELIN. Oh, Maria, my poor little Maria.

MARIA. No more Maria for you.

VATELIN. You really couldn't do a crazy thing like that.

MARIA. Then you come tonight, cuarenta-ocho Roo Ro-kay-pee-nay.

VATELIN. But I can't come to the Rue Roquépine tonight. What excuse could I give my wife?

MARIA. Then I suicide myself.

VATELIN. No! Don't say that! I'll meet you.

MARIA. And you luv me some more?

VATELIN. Yes, I love you again. (*HE holds his head in gesture of despair.*)

MARIA. I am very happy. I love you, Cray-peen.

VATELIN. I love you too, but I wish we were in Spain.

(*We hear the doorbell ring.*)

JEAN. (*appearing*) A gentleman is asking if you are in.

VATELIN. Who is it?

JEAN. Monsieur Soldignac.

MARIA. My husband!

VATELIN. Him! (*to JEAN*) Tell him I'll be with him in a moment. (*to MARIA*) Why did he come here?

MARIA. I doan know. I teenk he chess wan to say hello because he eez in Pa-rees.

VATELIN. In any case, he shouldn't see you. Go out

ACT I   THE FRENCH HAVE A WORD   45

this way. Run! (*indicates door at left, pushing her towards it*)

MARIA. Muy bien. Hasta esta noche!

VATELIN. All right—tonight.

MARIA. Forty-eight Roo Ro-kay-peenay.

VATELIN. Rue Roquépine. Yes, yes. Now go!

MARIA. You bad boy, Cray-peen—I luv you. You are my chinito! (*SHE kisses him warmly, then dashes out, left.*)

VATELIN. One mistake! And see what happens! I have deceived my wife only once and the whole world is caving in.

LUCIENNE. (*appearing at right door*) Has the woman gone?

VATELIN. Yes.

LUCIENNE. Who rang?

VATELIN. A friend that I knew in Madrid.

JEAN. (*bringing in SOLDIGNAC who is like an active volcano*) Monsieur Soldignac.

SOLDIGNAC. Good day my friend. How are you?

VATELIN. Very well. This is quite a surprise.

(*THEY shake hands.*)

VATELIN. Lucienne, this is Monsieur Soldignac.

LUCIENNE. I'm very pleased to meet you.

SOLDIGNAC. A pleasure for me. Oh, yes! (*sits*) My friend, I won't stay but a moment. I am very busy. But I wanted to shake your hand and also to speak to you about my wife.

VATELIN. (*seated at the desk*) Is Madame Soldignac well?

SOLDIGNAC. Very well. It is because of her that I have come. I have learned something that will astonish you.

My wife is deceiving me with another man.
VATELIN. What?
LUCIENNE. I'll leave the room if you wish.
SOLDIGNAC. No, it makes no difference. I am very philosophical. But this morning I found this letter in her wastebasket.
VATELIN. (*on pins and needles*) Does it name anyone?
SOLDIGNAC. No. But let me read it to you. (*reads*) "My love, I am in Paris. We can love each other again. This evening I will be alone at 48 Rue Roquépine. I will wait for you. Maria." (*looking up*) What do you say to that?
VATELIN. Well, one can't jump at conclusions. There may be nothing to it. Perhaps she is trying to make you jealous. Why would she throw the letter in the wastebasket?
SOLDIGNAC. I have no answer, but we'll see. I have talked to the police inspector, and tonight perhaps we'll catch the two together — my dear wife, and whoever "my love" happens to be.
VATELIN. You don't know how glad I am you told me this. I want to help.
SOLDIGNAC. You can help. I will get a divorce, and you can prepare all the necessary papers now, because I am in a hurry.
VATELIN. Of course you understand that your divorce depends on your catching your wife and her accomplice.
SOLDIGNAC. Naturally. But I am sure I will catch them tonight. And when I have the man in my hands, I will give him a few lessons in karate.
VATELIN. Are you good at that?
SOLDIGNAC. An expert. And my wife also. I taught her. I once fought the champion of Spain. Oh, I landed a blow that almost knocked him into Portugal.

VATELIN. Where did you hit him?
SOLDIGNAC. Right in the middle of Madrid. He didn't show his face in public for weeks.
VATELIN. It was quite a fight.
SOLDIGNAC. But wait until you see what I do to the man I catch tonight. (*HE does some make-believe karate chops very close to VATELIN's face, making him cringe.*) Au revoir, monsieur Vatelin, and Madame. (*HE goes out and bumps into PONTAGNAC coming in.*)
VATELIN. It's Pontagnac. (*to LUCIENNE*) Why don't you walk down with Monsieur Soldignac? I have something to say to Monsieur Pontagnac.

(*LUCIENNE goes out, rear*)

PONTAGNAC. Who was that demon?
VATELIN. A Frenchman who lives in Spain. You arrived at the right time, my friend. I have a favor to ask of you.
PONTAGNAC. Of me?
VATELIN. Yes—man to man. This evening I have a rendezvous with a woman.
PONTAGNAC. You? I'm thunderstruck.
VATELIN. You should be. So am I.
PONTAGNAC. You're deceiving your wife?
VATELIN. There are sometimes circumstances that force a man into it.
PONTAGNAC. You've come to the right person to reveal your secret. Proceed.
VATELIN. For various reasons it is going to be impossible for us to meet where we had planned. You're an old hand in this business, and I thought perhaps you could give me the name of a hotel where I could—
PONTAGNAC. Of course. Well, I use the Continental,

the Burgundy, the Ambassador, the Chatham and a few others, but of late I've been going to the Ultimus. It's very spacious and there are several exits. Also, the service is very good. But be sure to send word to them to reserve a room for tonight.

VATELIN. Thanks. I'll send a message immediately, and also one to the lady involved, so that she will be warned, and will ask for the room in my name.

PONTAGNAC. That's proper. But what about your wife? Will she give you liberty tonight?

VATELIN. My profession has its benefits. I'm often called out of town. I'll simply say that I'm called to open a will, or something like that. It will never be questioned.

PONTAGNAC. Perfect!

VATELIN. Excuse me while I send the message. (*HE goes out left.*)

PONTAGNAC. He's cheating on his wife. How glad I am to hear that.

LUCIENNE. (*comes from rear*) He was a strange one — that French Spaniard.

PONTAGNAC. Oh, Lucienne — come here quickly.

LUCIENNE. What is it?

PONTAGNAC. Well — well — no, I can't do it.

LUCIENNE. Can't do what?

PONTAGNAC. (*after a thoughtful moment*) Perhaps I can, after all. Love comes before everything.

LUCIENNE. Well?

PONTAGNAC. You said that if your husband ever deceived you, that you would do the same to him without hesitation.

LUCIENNE. Yes, I suppose I said that.

PONTAGNAC. Do you swear that you would act immediately if you had proof of his infidelity?

ACT I   THE FRENCH HAVE A WORD   49

LUCIENNE. Yes, immediately.

PONTAGNAC. I'm overjoyed. I have the proof! Tonight at the Hotel Ultimus your husband will be with a woman.

LUCIENNE. You're lying.

PONTAGNAC. Am I lying? In a few minutes he will tell you that he must leave the city in order to handle some legal matters – perhaps the opening of a will.

LUCIENNE. That isn't possible. Not Crépin.

PONTAGNAC. Yes – Crépin.

LUCIENNE. Could he be capable of it? Oh, if you just show me.

PONTAGNAC. Well, tonight I'll spy on him as he leaves, and I'll come in immediately and then lead you to the scene of the crime – the Hotel Ultimus. Are you willing?

LUCIENNE. Yes I'm willing.

PONTAGNAC. Quiet! Here he is. (*HE goes right.*)

VATELIN. (*entering left*) Oh, Lucienne, here you are. I have bad news.

LUCIENNE. Really? What is it?

VATELIN. A message that forces me to leave Paris this evening on the eight o'clock train. I have to go for the opening of a will.

LUCIENNE. Can't you have one of the clerks do it?

VATELIN. I wish that I could, but this client wants me personally.

LUCIENNE. Well, as they say: "Business is business".

VATELIN. Yes, unfortunately that's true, but I detest these annoying interruptions that take me away from you, if only for a few hours. Pardon me, I must get ready. (*goes out left, in a hurry*)

LUCIENNE. There goes the great deceiver – a real Tartuffe! (*SHE turns to PONTAGNAC.*) Were you about to say something?

PONTAGNAC. Only that I think you were well informed.

LUCIENNE. Oh, yes—your information was only too exact. And to think that I considered him a rare model of a husband. The liar! He's like all the others. Well, Monsieur Pontagnac, I shall be waiting for you, and I swear that when I find the proof that I need, I will be avenged within an hour.

PONTAGNAC. Oh, thank you! (*aside*) What a bastard I am! But for a good cause! (*to LUCIENNE*) Until tonight, Lucienne! (*HE goes out rear door.*)

LUCIENNE. (*going to her room, right, nervously agitated*) Until tonight!

THE FRENCH HAVE A WORD FOR IT

END OF ACT ONE

ACT TWO

THE FRENCH HAVE A WORD FOR IT

SCENE: *Room 39 at Hotel Ultimus. A large room, comfortably furnished. At rear in an alcove, is a bed. A table is in the middle of the room. Entry door is up left, giving onto a hallway. Down left is door that goes to room 38. There is a fireplace, and at right, a door leading to a bathroom. Other hotel furnishings. A trunk is near the fireplace. Candle in covered holder is on nightstand by bed.*

AT RISE: *ARMANDINE is standing by table, packing a handbag. Someone knocks at door.*

ARMANDINE. Come in!

(*VICTOR comes in, dressed in typical bellboy uniform and cap.*)

Oh, it's you, my young squirrel. Did you do what I told you to do?
    VICTOR. Yes, madame, yes. The manager said he would be here on the double.
    ARMANDINE. Did you speak to him about changing my room?

VICTOR. Yes, madame. He already knew, though. The chambermaid told him.

ARMANDINE. Thanks, sweetheart. Come here–closer.

VICTOR. Yes, madame.

ARMANDINE. How old are you?

VICTOR. Seventeen.

ARMANDINE. Seventeen. You're a good-looking boy.

VICTOR. (*lowering his head*) Oh, madame.

ARMANDINE. Don't be afraid. That should make you feel good, when I say you're good-looking.

VICTOR. Yes–it does–coming from you. (*HE closes his eyes, not daring to say more.*)

ARMANDINE. (*giving him a kiss on the cheek*) Well, I won't dispute that. You're a nice boy. (*After the kiss SHE rubs her hand across his face, and as SHE does, HE grabs her, bends her back in a rough and crude way, and plants a series of kisses on her face, neck and shoulders, then releases her as quickly.*)

ARMANDINE. What do you call that?

VICTOR. Oh, I beg your pardon, madame.

ARMANDINE. You're about as timid as a grizzly bear.

VICTOR. I didn't know what I was doing. I didn't hurt you, did I?

ARMANDINE. Not critically. There are certain sorts of roughness that don't hurt a woman.

VICTOR. You won't say anything to my boss, will you? He would kick me out.

ARMANDINE. (*laughs and sits on sofa*) That would be mean.

VICTOR. When I felt your warm hand on my cheek, I started trembling, and my head was spinning. I'm seventeen, and since I'm at seventeen some strange things have been happening. I get big pimples–almost boils. I've got one on my neck now. I showed it to a doctor who was in the hotel, and he said, "son, that's just puberty."

ARMANDINE. Puberty? What's that?

VICTOR. I don't know, but it seems that I'm old enough to make love. I can tell well enough that something is stirring up inside me. And sometimes at night—

ARMANDINE. Yes, I know about that.

VICTOR. Well, when you touched my cheek like that— you're not mad at me, are you?

ARMANDINE. (*rising*) Not at all. And to prove it, here are three francs.

VICTOR. (*with the money in his hand*) Three francs!

ARMANDINE. For you.

VICTOR. Oh, no, no, no. (*HE puts money on the table.*)

ARMANDINE. Why not?

VICTOR. Not from you, madame.

ARMANDINE. But, see here—

VICTOR. Oh, no! I would have paid *you* ten francs for—

ARMANDINE. For what?

VICTOR. For—(*HE is disturbed and is almost choking.*) For nothing, madame—I don't know what I mean. (*changing tone*) Here is the manager. (*As the manager comes in HE runs out.*)

MANAGER. Did Madame desire to talk to me?

ARMANDINE. Yes, about the room. I want to know what has been done. (*SHE has finished with her bag.*)

MANAGER. It's understood, madame, that you will have another room in the front.

ARMANDINE. Oh, yes, because it's dreary in here, and you know I must stay at least ten days while my new apartment is being readied for me.

MANAGER. I understand, madame.

ARMANDINE. Well, if it's not too much bother.

MANAGER. Of course not, Madame, provided that you will be willing to retain this room until this evening when I have it rented.

ARMANDINE. That's fine with me. Who is the lucky person that succeeds me?

MANAGER. A monsieur Vatelin who requested a reservation for this evening, and since I knew you wanted to change, I gave him this room.

ARMANDINE. Vatelin? I don't know him. But maybe that's better.

MANAGER. I will give madame number seventeen, facing the street.

ARMANDINE. Perfect, if you say so. All I need is a room large enough to accommodate a friend or other, just in case he wants to stay for the night.

MANAGER. Oh, madame will not be alone? You expect guests? Then perhaps I should give you room number twenty-eight. It has two beds.

ARMANDINE. Two beds? What the devil can I do in two beds? Are you joking with me?

MANAGER. But, madame—

ARMANDINE. Do you think I like an audience?

MANAGER. But, madame, I only thought that perhaps for madame's friend—

ARMANDINE. The other bed? He would throw a fit. No, I'll take number seventeen. (*SHE closes her bag.*)

MANAGER. Yes, madame. (*HE goes out, and we hear him speak to someone.*) Yes, monsieur, this is the room. (*HE comes back in.*) A gentleman for you, madame.

ARMANDINE. What gentleman?

MANAGER. I don't know. I'll ask him.

ARMANDINE. Don't bother. Have him come in.

MANAGER. Monsieur may come in.

(*HE leaves as REDILLON enters.*)

ARMANDINE. Oh, it's you.
REDILLON. You guessed. (*HE puts his hat down.*)
ARMANDINE. How have you been since I last saw you?
REDILLON. Very well. You're forgetting something.
ARMANDINE. What?

(*HE contracts his lips for a kiss and waits.*)

Oh, yes. (*SHE kisses him on the lips.*)
REDILLON. That was refreshing.
ARMANDINE. Do you still love me?
REDILLON. I adore you.
ARMANDINE. I've forgotten your name.
REDILLON. Ernest.
ARMANDINE. Ernest what? Or were you illegitimate?
REDILLON. No, I had a father. His name was Rédillon.
ARMANDINE. That's a stupid name.
REDILLON. It's all I have.
ARMANDINE. Well the name isn't what makes you a good lover. You're pretty, did you know that? And there's something else.
REDILLON. Oh, no.
ARMANDINE. You look like my lover.
REDILLON. Oh!
ARMANDINE. Didn't anyone ever tell you that?
REDILLON. No. Who is your lover?
ARMANDINE. He's a baron. Baron Schmitz-Mayer.
REDILLON. Who cares? Once more! (*once more purses his lips for a kiss, and SHE reciprocates*)
ARMANDINE. I knew right away that you were eyeing me at the theatre the other night.

REDILLON. Is that so?
ARMANDINE. Was that Pluplu with you in the box?
REDILLON. Yes. Do you know her?
ARMANDINE. Yes, I know her. And she knows me by sight. She's very chic. That's what made me want to know you. Otherwise I wouldn't have paid attention when you looked at me.
REDILLON. So I owe you to Pluplu?
ARMANDINE. Don't tell her so.
REDILLON. Don't be foolish. (*pulls her to him, with a new thought*) You're well put together—did you know? Does everything belong to you?
ARMANDINE. Who do you think it belongs to?
REDILLON. To me! All of it!

(THEY *kiss.*)

ARMANDINE. But you'll give it back to me, won't you?
REDILLON. Naturally.
ARMANDINE. Qui-qui wouldn't be happy if you didn't. Qui-qui is what I call my baron. [Kee-kee]
REDILLON. Stop talking about your stupid baron. Qui-qui! What a name.
ARMANDINE. It's no worse than Pluplu. And he loves me. He's so funny. He always says he loves me because I'm so stupid. Do you think I'm stupid?
REDILLON. If you are, you wear it very well. (*draws her to him*) My sweet Armandine.

(THEY *kiss.*)

ARMANDINE. My little—what was it?
REDILLON. Ernest.

ARMANDINE. I remembered – I just wanted to see if you did. My little Ernest.

REDILLON. (*sitting at L and pulling her on his knees*) Come sit on my knees.

ARMANDINE. Already?

REDILLON. Yes – already. (*embraces her*) Oh, my dear Lucienne.

ARMANDINE. Lucienne? My name isn't Lucienne. It's Armandine.

REDILLON. No! Lucienne! Let me call you Lucienne. What does it matter? I just happen to like that name. Oh, Lucienne.

ARMANDINE. You're funny. That reminds me of one time when I –

REDILLON. Don't let me remind you of anything. Just keep quiet. Don't talk, just kiss me. Oh, Lucienne, it's really you, Lucienne.

ARMANDINE. No, it isn't.

REDILLON. Quiet! I didn't tell you to answer. Tell me it's you, Lucienne.

(*knock at door*)

ARMANDINE. Who is there?

VICTOR'S VOICE. It's Victor, madame – the bell boy.

ARMANDINE. Oh, it's you. Come in.

VICTOR. (*entering*) Madame, may I – ? (*scandalized, seeing her on REDILLON's knees*) Oh!

ARMANDINE. What is it, my little one?

VICTOR. (*tenderly*) Madame, I want to know if I may take your trunk.

ARMANDINE. Yes, yes.

REDILLON. (*to VICTOR*) Which trunk?

VICTOR. (*brutally*) That trunk – there. Not the king of Sweden's.

REDILLON. (*rising and going to VICTOR*) Where did you learn to talk like that? I'm going to teach you if it was the King of Sweden's or not.

ARMANDINE. Don't you hurt him! He's a nice boy.

REDILLON. I didn't say he wasn't. I just want to teach him to speak politely.

ARMANDINE. Don't bother. Give him five francs.

REDILLON. What? After the way he –?

ARMANDINE. Do you refuse to give him five francs for me? (*SHE sits at left.*)

REDILLON. The five francs have nothing to do with it. (*hands five francs to VICTOR*) Here's five francs for this time, but it won't happen again. (*HE goes R.*)

VICTOR. (*dryly*) Thank you. Pig!

REDILLON. (*not hearing*) That's the way I am!

VICTOR. (*with tender voice to ARMANDINE*) Madame, I'm going to look for the chambermaid so she can help me carry your trunk.

ARMANDINE. (*seated L*) Yes, you do that, little one.

(*VICTOR leaves.*)

REDILLON. At least he'll know that it costs him money to be impolite.

ARMANDINE. Don't be angry at the boy. He's nervous because he's very sick.

REDILLON. I don't give a damn if he's sick.

ARMANDINE. But if you knew what he had –

REDILLON. What does he have?

ARMANDINE. He has a very bad case of puberty.

REDILLON. Puberty? What do you mean, puberty?

ACT II THE FRENCH HAVE A WORD 59

ARMANDINE. That's what he has. A doctor told him so.

REDILLON. Is that his sickness? Really, I feel sorry for him.

ARMANDINE. Is it serious?

REDILLON. Puberty? It certainly is.

ARMANDINE. It isn't catching is it?

REDILLON. Unfortunately no. If it were, he could make a fortune passing it around.

VICTOR. (*entering, speaks to CLARA behind him*) Help me.

CLARA. (*entering*) This trunk?

VICTOR. Yes. We have to take it to room seventeen. (*taking small bag from table*) And this bag.

(*THEY carry off the trunk and bag.*)

REDILLON. Are you moving?

ARMANDINE. Yes. I don't like this room. I asked for one on the street.

REDILLON. Well, let's go to the new room. (*takes his hat*)

ARMANDINE. Both of us? What for?

REDILLON. What for? You *are* stupid.

ARMANDINE. NO, no – not tonight.

REDILLON. Why not?

ARMANDINE. It's impossible, that's why. A thousand pardons.

REDILLON. Do you think you're going to leave me here dangling on a string like a puppet?

ARMANDINE. There is simply no way. I'm waiting for a friend at eleven o'clock.

REDILLON. A friend? Do you call that a reason? Who

is it?

ARMANDINE. A man from Spain. You don't know him. His name is Soldignac. Every time he comes to Paris he—

REDILLON. (*cutting in*) Never mind the details. It's disgusting.

ARMANDINE. Just the same, he'll be here.

REDILLON. But you don't have to be here. Come to my humble abode.

ARMANDINE. Yours?

REDILLON. (*taking her arm*) Yes, mine. I have a home. Did you think I slept under a bridge?

ARMANDINE. But what shall I tell my friend?

REDILLON. You don't tell him anything. You just leave word that you are sorry, but you had to sit up with your sick grandmother. That's always a good excuse.

ARMANDINE. That's not nice.

REDILLON. Of course it is. Come angel, put on your hat and I'll take you there.

ARMANDINE. (*goes to get hat at fireplace*) It's a rotten thing to do, but it tempts me. I think I'll do it!

(*There is a knock at the door.*)

MANAGER. (*enters*) Pardon me for disturbing you, but the guests who reserved this room are here, and so—

ARMANDINE. And so you would like us kindly to remove our carcasses.

MANAGER. I would never put it that way.

ARMANDINE. As soon as I put on my hat, you can have the place, so tell Monsieur—what's his name?

MANAGER. Vatelin.

REDILLON. Vatelin?

ARMANDINE. Tell him to give me one minute.
REDILLON. Is Vatelin here? What luck. Have him come in. I want to shake his hand.
ARMANDINE. Do you know him?
REDILLON. I know him better than anyone.
MANAGER. (*to PINCHARD outside*) Monsieur can come in.
REDILLON. (*rushing to door, hand extended*) Ah, my dear friend.

(*PINCHARD dressed as army medical major, comes in, followed by wife.*)

Oh, excuse me, it's not the same Vatelin.
PINCHARD. (*to REDILLON and ARMANDINE, while his wife bows and scrapes*) I'm terribly sorry to dislodge you, monsieur and madame. (*seperately to ARMANDINE*) You're pretty. (*HE hands his handbag to wife who puts it on table, and then rejoins them.*) I sent a telegram to reserve a room for tonight, and as you can see by this answer–(*reads from telegram*) "Reserving room thirty-nine for you." (*looks up*) so this is the room. (*PINCHARD is always calm, almost dense, but rough and aggressive.*)
ARMANDINE. (*putting on gloves*) But we should apologize for still being here. We were just going to leave.
PINCHARD. Please, Madame, take your time. I don't like bothering anyone in the slightest. If there is room for two here, there is room for four.
ARMANDINE. You are very kind.
PINCHARD. Not at all. (*to REDILLON*) I compliment you, Monsieur. You have a handsome wife.

(*REDILLON nods approval.*)

I'll be glad to trade mine for yours.

(REDILLON and ARMANDINE, astonished, look at MADAME PINCHARD who is all smiles, and makes little bows and other gestures.)

Oh, I'm not afraid of saying it in front of my wife.
  REDILLON. Doesn't she mind?
  PINCHARD. It's not that she doesn't mind, but she's as deaf as a post.

(REDILLON and ARMANDINE muffle a laugh.)

  MADAME PINCHARD. Please don't put yourself to any trouble on our account.
  ARMANDINE. Yes, that's what your husband just had the kindness to say to us.
  MADAME PINCHARD. (*who didn't get a word of it*) Oh, yes, I think so too.
  PINCHARD. Does that make sense to you?
  REDILLON. No.
  PINCHARD. To me either. What she replies is always a little incoherent because she doesn't hear the question.
  MADAME PINCHARD. My husband also!
  PINCHARD. You see! You have to put up with it. I have, for twenty-five years. We've been married twenty-five years today, and that's why we're in Paris. We'll celebrate our anniversary by going to the Opera.
  REDILLON. Opera? Are you going this evening?
  PINCHARD. Yes. It's a little late but we like to arrive just in time for the ballet, because singing bores me, and my wife can't hear it. But she enjoys watching the dancers in the ballet. But she says ballet would be better if it

had music. (*giving his wife a little tap on the arm*) Isn't that so, Coco?

MADAME PINCHARD. What?

PINCHARD. (*puts thumb of each hand in pockets of his jacket and taps on his stomach with the other fingers*) You think the ballets are lacking in music?

MADAME PINCHARD. It's much better now, but it was bothering me on the train.

(*REDILLON and ARMANDINE look at each other.*)

PINCHARD. She's talking about her stomach. She gets little attacks — I don't know just what causes them. But she's better now. You'll find her talk disconnected, but you soon get used to it.

ARMANDINE. We won't disturb you any longer. Are you ready, Ernest?

REDILLON. Yes, but I want to tell Monsieur something before I leave.

PINCHARD. What's that?

REDILLON. One of my best friends is named Vatelin.

PINCHARD. (*completely confused*) Oh?

REDILLON. Yes.

PINCHARD. Well, one confidence is worth another. My best friend is named Napoleon.

REDILLON. (*equally confused*) Oh?

PINCHARD. Delighted to have met you.

REDILLON. Monsieur! (*turns to MADAME*) Madame!

(*MADAME PINCHARD doesn't budge.*)

PINCHARD. (*giving her a tap on the arm*) Coco! Monsieur and Madame want to say good-bye.

MADAME PINCHARD. What?

PINCHARD. Monsieur and Madame want to say good-bye.

MADAME PINCHARD. I can't hear you.

PINCHARD. Wait a minute. (*HE looks directly at his wife, moves his lips to form the following words without uttering a sound.*) Monsieur-and-Madame-want-to-tell-you-good-bye.

MADAME PINCHARD. Oh, pardon. Good-bye, monsieur. Good-bye, madame.

REDILLON. (*to ARMANDINE*) That's curious. She only hears him when we can't hear him at all.

ARMANDINE. Shall we go now?

(*There is a knock at the door.*)

ARMANDINE. Come in.

VICTOR. (*entering*) Has Madame anything more to be moved?

ARMANDINE. No, thank you, Victor. But you can tell them at the reception that if a man asks for me, they should tell him that I have not been able to wait for him because I was called to take care of my grandmother who is very ill.

VICTOR. Yes, madame.

ARMANDINE. Take care of your health, little one.

PINCHARD. Is he sick?

ARMANDINE. Yes, he's bothered with boils. Take care of yourself. (*as REDILLON follows her to go out*) Oh, my bag.

REDILLON. Oh, yes. (*to VICTOR*) Her bag, there on the table.

VICTOR. Yes, monsieur. (*HE takes PINCHARD's bag*

from table and hands it to REDILLON.)
REDILLON. That's it. (*HE goes out behind ARMANDINE.*)
MADAME PINCHARD. I'll get ready so we can go to the Opera. (*SHE goes into bathroom.*)

PINCHARD. (*to VICTOR*) Well, don't just stand there like a stump in the ground.
VICTOR. Monsieur!
PINCHARD. So you have boils.
VICTOR. Yes, Major, but they're not serious.
PINCHARD. I'm the one to judge that. I'm Major in the Medical Corps of the Cavalry. Drop your trousers.
VICTOR. What?
PINCHARD. You heard me. Drop your trousers!

(*MADAME PINCHARD comes in.*)

VICTOR. But, Major.
PINCHARD. Don't worry about my wife. She's deaf.
VICTOR. Oh! (*starts to undo his belt, then hesitates*)
PINCHARD. Well, I'm waiting.
VICTOR. I just want to say that if you're just curious, I'll take down my trousers, but if it's for the boil – well, it's on my neck.
PINCHARD. On your neck? What are yelling about, then? That doesn't count. That won't keep you from riding a horse. (*marches on VICTOR, angrily*) Soldier, I ought to kick you in the ass.
VICTOR. But, Major –
PINCHARD. Out – on the double – or faster than that.
VICTOR. Yes, Major. (*HE dashes out of the room.*)
PINCHARD. Did you ever hear of such a thing? A boil

on the neck?

MADAME PINCHARD. No! It's ten-thirty, dear. You just have enough time.

PINCHARD. I wasn't talking about that. I was talking about a boil on the neck that should have been on his rear end.

MADAME PINCHARD. Look at the program, dear. It will tell you.

PINCHARD. I'm going to get ready. Where is my bag?

MADAME PINCHARD. What?

PINCHARD. (*moving lips without a sound*) Where-is-my-bag?

MADAME PINCHARD. How do I know? You were carrying it?

PINCHARD. Was I carrying it? (*seeing SHE doesn't understand HE talks with lips*) Was-I-carrying-it?

MADAME PINCHARD. Yes. Where did you put it?

PINCHARD. That's a good question. Where could I have hidden it?

(*There is a knock at door.*)

Come in.

(*PINCHARD and MADAME are looking for the bag.*)

CLARA. I came to make the bed. Are you looking for something?

PINCHARD. Yes – a handbag. Where the devil did I put it?

MADAME PINCHARD. See if the bellboy carried it to the bathroom.

PINCHARD. I would have seen him. But I'll look. (*HE*

goes into bathroom.)

CLARA. Does Madame prefer a feather pillow or a hair pillow?

(*silence from MADAME*)

Does Madame prefer a feather pillow or a hair pillow? (*confused*) What's the matter with her? She's in the clouds. (*going right up to MADAME*) Does Madame prefer—

MADAME PINCHARD. Oh, yes, dearie, I'm quite comfortable here. (*SHE goes left, CLARA following.*)

CLARA. I was asking if—

(*PINCHARD enters.*)

PINCHARD. Don't ask her anything—you're wasting your time. What did you want of her?

CLARA. I wanted to know—

PINCHARD. (*whistles*) You're a very nice dish.

CLARA. I wanted to know what kind of pillow you preferred. Feathers or hair?

PINCHARD. You're not only pretty, but you're put together like a brick barracks.

CLARA. I was only asking—

PINCHARD. Who gives a damn what's in the pillows? I'd like one half of a pillow like you have, you sweet thing. (*HE tries to lay his head against her breast.*)

CLARA. (*scandalized*) Monsieur!

PINCHARD. What's your name?

CLARA. You don't need to know.

(*HE tries to pinch her behind as SHE is working on bed.*)

Madame, will you please make your husband stop.
  PINCHARD. Call her! Yell at her!
  CLARA. Will you tell your husband to leave me alone?
  MADAME PINCHARD. Yes, we'll be here until tomorrow, dearie.
  CLARA. She's deaf.
  PINCHARD. Deaf as a scarecrow. But you're pretty. (*HE kisses her and SHE slaps him and goes right.*)
  MADAME PINCHARD. Well, have you got it?
  PINCHARD. (*holding his cheek*) I got it all right.
  CLARA. Does Monsieur desire anything else?
  PINCHARD. No thanks! You're as strong as a female gorilla.
  MADAME PINCHARD. Have you got a toothache?
  PINCHARD. No – it's nothing. (*to CLARA*) Tell them at reception to bring my bag up if I left it down there. (*HE takes his cap and puts his on.*)
  CLARA. Very well, Monsieur. (*SHE goes to the bed.*)
  PINCHARD. Come on, Coco, (*without voice*) Let's-go-Coco.
  MADAME PINCHARD. I'm ready.

(*THEY go out.*)

  CLARA. (*to audience*) I think I cooled the Major's pipes. He says he would like to have half of my pillow, but so does the man in room twenty-three, and forty-seven, and thirty-four, and ten or twelve others. Does he really believe that I would be in here making beds and cleaning bathrooms if I wanted to be a whore? Men are stupid!
  PONTAGNAC. (*head half through doorway up left, carrying a package*) If I'm not mistaken, I heard them leave this room. Vatelin should be here soon. It's time to in-

stall the communications system. (*tiptoes to door left*)
CLARA. What were you asking for, Monsieur?
PONTAGNAC. Oh, the maid!
CLARA. Were you looking for someone?
PONTAGNAC. Yes. The King of Bulgaria.
CLARA. He's not here.
PONTAGNAC. Not here? The devil! It's as I suspected.
CLARA. Well, then—
PONTAGNAC. I'm sure he was in Room Thirty-nine, but I was wondering if this is the hotel.
CLARA. Yes, you could be mistaken about that.
PONTAGNAC. I saw the King today, and he said: "My good friend, we'll be at the Ultimus, room thirty-nine." So, I'm certain about the room, but I could have been mistaken about the hotel—because of his accent, you see. Instead of Ultimus, he might have said Hotel Blanche Fontaine or Hotel Royal Malesherbes.
CLARA. Are you in the king's court?
PONTAGNAC. Indeed I am. I'm chief minister in charge of bombings and assassinations. I must always be near the king, so I reserved room thirty-eight. (*approaching left door*) Room thirty-eight is there, isn't it?
CLARA. It should be, since this is room thirty-nine.

(*PONTAGNAC is already at the door, trying to get the key out of the lock, as CLARA works at the bed.*)

PONTAGNAC. (*HE has the key in his hand.*) Well, he's not here, and there's no more to be said. Good evening. (*HE goes out quickly.*)
CLARA. That's funny! He can't find his king. But I'm going to have to find some pillows. (*SHE goes out.*)

(*We hear a key in door at left and then PONTAGNAC enters, followed by LUCIENNE.*)

PONTAGNAC. Don't be afraid—there's no one here.
LUCIENNE. So this is the room.
PONTAGNAC. Number thirty-nine—that's right.
LUCIENNE. (*sits*) What turpitude. And to think it will happen in this room. The room looks honest enough, but it lies. But it's in this room that my husband will soon be appearing.
PONTAGNAC. With a woman.
LUCIENNE. (*rising*) Yes! Then, the two of them—the man I have known intimately—with his words and his tenderness-and a woman I don't even know—with her—with her—I don't know what! (*SHE gets emotional.*) I can't do it. I won't do it. How can you stand by, in cold blood, and watch this going on?
PONTAGNAC. But what if it's a beautiful gesture?
LUCIENNE. Don't say it! I see only too well now, and I see myself. Frightful images come before my eyes. No, I don't want to see it! (*puts her hands over her eyes*) But that doesn't help. I see the images even more vividly when I close my eyes.
PONTAGNAC. Please, don't get yourself into a nervous state.
LUCIENNE. I'm beginning to hate everyone around me. And everything around me. These walls are accomplices. These chairs are silent witnesses. I won't have it! I won't! Where is the bell?
PONTAGNAC. The bell?
LUCIENNE. To call someone.
PONTAGNAC. What for?
LUCIENNE. I'm going to tell them to remove this bed.

I want this bed out of here!

PONTAGNAC. But you can't do that. Do you want to surprise your husband or not?

LUCIENNE. Of course I want to surprise him.

PONTAGNAC. Well, if you want evidence that a game has been played, don't take away the playing field.

LUCIENNE. But the kind of proof you suggest is horrible.

PONTAGNAC. We'll try to make the game as short as possible.

LUCIENNE. Yes, yes.

PONTAGNAC. We'll surprise them at the psychological moment.

LUCIENNE. That may be too late. Before that!

PONTAGNAC. I know what you mean, but we can't arrive before the violins are tuned up, and we must certainly arrive before—

LUCIENNE. Before the concert begins.

PONTAGNAC. Exactly. We must arrive on the up-beat.

LUCIENNE. But how shall we know?

PONTAGNAC. Well, I've given great throught to it, and I think I have a perfect plan. (*HE shows two electric bells that operate on batteries that were in the package HE was carrying.*)

LUCIENNE. What are they? Bells?

PONTAGNAC. Electric bells. They're used in fishing.

LUCIENNE. Fishing?

PONTAGNAC. Yes. You put one of these bells on the end of your line, and the fish rings the bell to let you know that he's been caught. I simply applied the method to Vatelin.

LUCIENNE. So you're going to catch my husband as you would a fish?

PONTAGNAC. That's right. Your husband and his – his – companion – will be the ones to ring the bells to let us know the exact moment to surprise them.

LUCIENNE. It sounds stupid.

PONTAGNAC. Fish are fooled by it, and men are just as stupid as fish. You'll see how easy it is. (*HE goes to the bed, and LUCIENNE trails behind.*) Which side of the bed does your husband usually take?

LUCIENNE. Let me think. (*SHE sizes up the bed, but can't decide, goes into alcove, points to side by wall.*) I believe I'm always on this side.

PONTAGNAC. (*HE sits on edge of bed, on side facing audience.*) Then Vatelin is on this side?

LUCIENNE. I think so.

PONTAGNAC. (*HE turns towards her.*) You must be sure.

LUCIENNE. (*coming out of alcove*) I'm sure!

(*PONTAGNAC gets off the bed.*)

PONTAGNAC. So, we'll put the baritone bell on this side. (*HE rings the bell and it has a low sound.*) We'll say this is Vatelin. And the other – (*HE rings the other bell which has a sharp sound.*) will be the woman. (*rings them alternately*) Monsieur! Madame! Monsieur! Madame! (*HE puts one bell under mattress at side of bed where HE had been lying.*) I place Monsieur here. (*HE places other bell on the opposite side of the bed, by the wall.*) And Madame here.

LUCIENNE. Now what?

PONTAGNAC. (*still inside the alcove*) Now what? That's all for now. The bait is set. Now we have to wait for the fish to bite. When we hear one bell, we won't budge, because only one fish is swimming by, but when we hear the second bell, we know we have two fish.

LUCIENNE. You're very clever.

PONTAGNAC. I'm a genius, that's all. (*hears a noise*) But I hear someone. It might be our fish.

LUCIENNE. I'm going to scratch out the eyes of that mackerel and his trout.

PONTAGNAC. They're not here yet and you already want to scratch out their eyes. Come now, we haven't got much time. (*HE goes to door left.*)

LUCIENNE. (*raising fist towards rear door*) I'll catch you yet, Vatelin. (*SHE follows PONTAGNAC out left. An instant afterwards the rear door opens and MARIA comes in, followed by CLARA who holds two pillows.*)

MARIA. I ask for treinta-nueve. Is thees room for monsee-oor Vatelin? (*puts her bag on table*)

CLARA. But I told you, Madame, when guests are absent, I can't allow anyone in their room without a special order.

MARIA. (*sitting by table*) Cállate, ya has hablado bastante! I tole you he say to wait if he not here. He send me telegram. Here, if you no believe – read – you know how read?

CLARA. Sí.

MARIA. Oh, you speak the Spanish.

CLARA. Sí. That's all I know is "sí". (*reading the telegram*) "Your husband knows everything. He found your letter in the wastebasket." (*interrupting*) Oh, ho!

MARIA. (*rises and grabs telegram*) Hey! You read my private part! You jess read the end, thass all. (*looking at telegram*) "Come to Hotel Ultimush." (*hands her telegram*) Here! Read last line.

CLARA. (*reading*) "Ask for my room, and if I'm not there, wait for me." Signed, Vatelin.

MARIA. *(takes telegram and then starts pulling things from her handbag which she puts on table)* Well, are you conwinched?

CLARA. Sí.

MARIA. *(who has a dressing gown in her hand)* Where is the bat-room?

CLARA. This way, Madame. *(SHE opens bathroom door at right.)*

MARIA. *(holding up her robe as a Toreador holds his cape.)* Olé! *(SHE goes into bathroom as VICTOR comes in with VATELIN, carrying bag.)*

VICTOR. This is your room, Monsieur.

VATELIN. Good!

CLARA. But you must have made a mistake, Victor. This room is already taken by Monsieur Vatelin.

VATELIN. I'm Monsieur Vatelin.

CLARA. But what about the Major and his wife who were here just a while ago?

VATELIN. *(putting his bag on sofa)* Don't worry about it, mademoiselle. They told me downstairs about the mistake. There was an error in a telegram, and the couple who were to have room fifty-nine were put in room thirty-nine. But it's all straightened out now, and the couple will be notified when they return.

CLARA. Sí!

VATELIN. What?

CLARA. I mean "yes". I understand.

VATELIN. Thank you. Bellboy, this is for you. *(HE gives VICTOR a coin.)* And please tell them at reception that if someone asks for me, give them my room number and send them up.

VICTOR. Yes, monsieur. Right away. *(HE rushes out.)*

CLARA. Is monsieur looking for a woman?

VATELIN. No thanks – I already have more than I can use.

CLARA. Beg pardon, but I wasn't offering one to you. But there was a woman asking for you, and she's here now.

VATELIN. She is? Already?

CLARA. Shall I tell her you're here?

VATELIN. No. She'll find me too soon by herself. Why don't you bring us two cups of coffee? (*CLARA leaves.*) I hope she takes a long, long time in making her appearance. I'm not in a very good mood.

(*VATELIN has his back to bathroom door, as MARIA in sexy dressing gown, opens door, sees VATELIN, and comes from behind to cover his eyes with her hands.*)

MARIA. Guess who?

VATELIN. I can't guess.

MARIA. You geev up? It is Maria, your luv.

VATELIN. I was afraid of that.

MARIA. Oh, Cray-peen, I am so happy. (*SHE lets go and then stands looking at him.*) Why you stand there like a gas burner?

VATELIN. A gas burner?

MARIA. Like a beeg, tall gas burner.

VATELIN. What are you talking about?

MARIA. You know – the beeg gas burner in the street.

VATELIN. Do you mean lamp post?

MARIA. Lamp post. Why you stand there like a lamp post? Doan you wan kiss me?

VATELIN. No!

MARIA. No? Caramba! Madre de Dios! You say "no"?

VATELIN. Let me explain. You wanted me to come here so I came. It was the only way I could prevent your blowing your brains out. Let me rephrase that—blowing your head off. I gave in to your whim, but if you are able to reason things out in a clear manner, you must know that everything is finished between us.

MARIA. Oh, Cray-peen, why do you say such hor-ee-bul things to me. Estás malo, muy malo.

VATELIN. I don't know what "malo" means, but I'm sure it suits me.

MARIA. I was loving you because you are tender and refined. My husband, he is a big brute—a pig.

VATELIN. Who cares? Is that the only reason you loved me?

MARIA. But you know how to treat a woman.

VATELIN. Me? You're all wrong. Do you think I'm tender and refined? I break women into little pieces. I'm a man who ruins fifty women a year. I demolish them! I use them! I throw them away! I'm straight out of the underworld of Paris. (*VATELIN does ridiculous Apache movements, left hand striking behind his neck, right hand before his face, striking into space.*)

MARIA. (*sits*) Oh, you are funny like that. Me gusta.

VATELIN. Get off your butt, chicken! You think I'm funny? Let me tell you—I'm as funny as a rattlesnake. Oh, you don't know me at all. I'm not good, and I'm not sweet, and I'm not tender. When I was in Spain, I was a visitor, but in France, I'm myself—and I'm bad, rotten, mean, all the way through—brutal, violent, tough!

MARIA. You?

VATELIN. Yes—me! I'd as soon knock down a woman as a man. (*a false crazy laugh*) Ha, ha, ha, ha! (*assumes an aggressive boxer's stance*)

MARIA. (*laughing furiously*) Oh, Cray-peen.
VATELIN. Don't come near or I'll chop you into bits.
MARIA. Qué dices?
VATELIN. Huh?
MARIA. What you say?
VATELIN. I said don't come near me or I'll destroy you.
MARIA. Estás loco en la cabeza!
VATELIN. You heard me. Be warned.
MARIA. Try something, tonto! (*SHE assumes a defensive position.*)
VATELIN. (*giving her an insignificant push with flat of his hand*) There!

(*MARIA giggles but does not move.*)

MARIA. What you call that? A love pat? (*With a yell, SHE gives him a quick karate chop to neck, with right hand then left hand, then with both hands together to his stomach. HE bends over, holding his stomach and SHE gives him a sharp blow on back of neck.*) You still wan to fight?

(*VATELIN is on the floor.*)

VATELIN. Enough! Oh, la, la!
MARIA. You dirty Frenchmen, you doan know how fight except with your feet. (*SHE then goes to him and kisses him.*) Oh, Cray-peen, I luv you.

(*a knock at the door*)

Come in!

CLARA. (*entering with tray, coffee, sugar etc.*) Here's your coffee.

MARIA. Muchas gracias.

CLARA. Sí. (*SHE leaves. MARIA sits on chair, right of table.*)

MARIA. You got good beating. You wan make luv or you wan fight some more?

VATELIN. You took advantage of me.

MARIA. You see you got to be nice to me. Entiendes, burro?

VATELIN. Can't anything stop you? Don't you realize that your husband has a bug in his ear?

MARIA. Doan you talk about my husband. Who tole you he has bugs?

VATELIN. No, no – that's an expression – an idiom. It means that someone has told him that you have a lover in Paris. If I hadn't sent you that telegram –

MARIA. Oh, yes. I would have jumped into the lion's ear.

VATELIN. You mean the lion's mouth. That's right, and so you see, I can't go on with this little affair, and you should realize that. So, good-bye. Adios!

MARIA. Cray-peen, Cray-peen, stay here!

VATELIN. No, Maria – let me go.

MARIA. No! Nunca!

VATELIN. You must let me go.

MARIA. If you go, I suicide myself.

VATELIN. Again? That's blackmail! Go on – get hysterical – but leave me alone.

MARIA. Muy bien. I drink my coffee and then I die.

VATELIN. All right – then die.

MARIA. You will take a cup of coffee?

VATELIN. If you wish.

MARIA. Two sugars or one sugars?
VATELIN. Four. (*HE sits at table.*)
MARIA. (*taking a small bottle from her pocket*) One drops or two drops?
VATELIN. I don't care—give me a spoonful.
MARIA. That's too much.
VATELIN. I'm a gourmet.
MARIA. But a spoonful will keel a army.
VATELIN. (*pushing away spoon and rising*) What is that stuff, anyhow?
MARIA. Streak-a-nine. (*SHE caries the bottle to her lips.*)
VATELIN. Strychnine? Give me that! (*HE falls on her, trying to get the bottle.*)
MARIA. No! I wan drink, and suicide myself in front of both your eyes.
VATELIN. In the name of heaven—give me that.
MARIA. No, Cray-peen. Adios!

(*THEY struggle in a routine that is almost like an Apache dance.*)

VATELIN. Maria, I'll be kind. I'll do anything you ask.
MARIA. You just say that.
VATELIN. I swear it.
MARIA. Sí?
VATELIN. Sí.
MARIA. That's better. (*SHE puts the bottle in her pocket.*)
VATELIN. You're right, Maria. We shouldn't be fighting. I love you—I want you—come to me. (*HE takes her in his arms and tries to get her into the bed.*)
MARIA. (*pulls away*) Oh, no, Cray-peen—not like that.

VATELIN. (*assuming the Apache role again*) But, my chicken, you know what I want.

MARIA. Yes, I want too.

VATELIN. Then why are you throwing cold water on my enthusiasm?

MARIA. (*putting hand on his mouth*) Be quiet! Shut up! Cállate! I love you—you love us.

VATELIN. Yes.

MARIA. Then I go change into something more pretty for making love.

VATELIN. Why don't you change here?

MARIA. Dat's not nice! No—you wait—you see. (*SHE goes out right, into bathroom.*)

VATELIN. How am I going to get out of this! (*sits on bed and the bell rings*) Did I hear a bell?

(*A quick silent scene follows as LUCIENNE opens door at L and sticks in her head. Recognizing her husband, SHE raises both arms and opens her mouth in protest. But PONTAGNAC grabs her and pulls her back into the room while holding the door open, then closing it.*)

(*VATELIN rises, bell stops ringing*) Huh? Nobody is there. But I heard a bell. (*goes to inspect door at left*) Locked! Oh, it's all the fault of Maria and her strychnine flavored coffee. I'm going to have them take out that tray. (*reading on wall*) "Chambermaid, two rings." (*HE rings twice and hears a knock at door.*) That was quick. Come in.

SOLDIGNAC. (*entering*) Good evening.

VATELIN. Soldignac! It's you.

SOLDIGNAC. Yes, it is I.

ACT II   THE FRENCH HAVE A WORD

VATELIN. What are you doing here?

SOLDIGNAC. (*going to table*) That intrigues you, doesn't it?

VATELIN. Hardly.

SOLDIGNAC. I was downstairs at reception when the bellboy came with your message: "if anyone asks for Vatelin have them come to room thirty-nine."

(*VATELIN tries to block bathroom door, but SOLDIGNAC takes his arm and they execute some movements as VATELIN goes for bathroom door again, and SOLDIGNAC tries to walk with him.*)

What do you think – I was to meet a woman here tonight in this very room. She wasn't able to wait for me. She left word that her grandmother was sick. (*stops and looks at VATELIN*) That doesn't seem to interest you very much. (*HE lets go of his arm.*)

VATELIN. Oh, yes. I heard you say "sick". Are you sick?

SOLDIGNAC. Who?

VATELIN. You.

SOLDIGNAC. No! She is. I mean her grandmother.

VATELIN. That's too bad. Her grandmother?

SOLDIGNAC. Yes. I wonder what I should do. Should I leave?

VATELIN. (*quickly shoves him to door*) I hate to see you leave, but if you must, please go.

SOLDIGNAC. I really can't go yet. Since I knew that I would be at the hotel tonight, I made an appointment with the Police Inspector.

VATELIN. Police Inspector?

SOLDIGNAC. I told you that I was going to try to catch

my wife in the act tonight.

VATELIN. But she's not here! She's not here!

SOLDIGNAC. You mean my wife? I know that. She's at forty-eight Rue Roquépine.

VATELIN. Oh, I'm glad to hear that.

SOLDIGNAC. Huh?

VATELIN. I mean, I'm relieved that you know where she is.

SOLDIGNAC. The detective is probably catching her at this very moment.

VATELIN. (*goes near door right*) Yes, yes, yes.

SOLDIGNAC. So as not to make a mistake, he's been trailing her all day. (*looks at VATELIN*) You don't seem to be interested in what I'm saying.

VATELIN. Of course I am. You said she was sick.

SOLDIGNAC. No, she's not sick now – that was before – and it was her grandmother.

VATELIN. She's not sick now? Do you mean she's dead?

SOLDIGNAC. No, no, no! No more sick grandmother. That was about the girl I was to meet. Now I'm talking about my wife.

VATELIN. Your wife who is here?

SOLDIGNAC. No, no, no! My wife is not here. She's at Rue Roquépine.

VATELIN. Oh, yes.

SOLDIGNAC. The police inspector is going to send word to me here that the case is closed.

VATELIN. Oh, that's perfect, that's perfect. (*HE shows his agitation.*)

SOLDIGNAC. Why are you so nervous?

VATELIN. I'm not nervous. Do I look nervous?

SOLDIGNAC. Yes. I think you're ill.

VATELIN. (*his thumbs in pockets of vest*) No, no. Well, I may be slightly ill.
SOLDIGNAC. Sit down.
VATELIN. I don't want to sit down.
SOLDIGNAC. Then I'll sit down. (*HE sits on sofa.*)
VATELIN. Good God!

(*At this moment the door at right opens and MARIA's arm is thrust through and throws her bodice on the chair by the door.*)

SOLDIGNAC. (*who sees her arm*) Very pretty – very pretty.
VATELIN. (*who just now has seen the arm*) Did you see that? Do you know what that was? (*HE is petrified.*) That was an arm.
SOLDIGNAC. A very lovely arm. Oh, you lover boy. Whose arm is it? (*HE puts his hat on the table.*)
VATELIN. I don't know. It doesn't belong *here*. I don't know where it came from. Probably from the room next door.
SOLDIGNAC. Faker! It was your wife's arm.
VATELIN. That's right – it was your wife's arm. (*aghast*) I mean *my* wife's arm. I mean the arm of the woman next door. (*HE picks up the blouse that MARIA threw in, but at that moment the arm appears again, holding MARIA's skirt. VATELIN grabs it quickly, wads it up with the blouse and stuffs all of it under the bed.*)
SOLDIGNAC. Where did you go, my friend?
VATELIN. Here I am.
SOLDIGNAC. Sit down here so we can talk.
VATELIN. (*sitting on sofa arm*) I'm sitting.

SOLDIGNAC. My compliments. Your wife has a fine arm.

(*At this moment MARIA enters directly into the scene. SHE has on nothing but her undergarments, and a little boudoir cap on her head. When she sees her husband, SHE utters a muffled cry and rushes back into the bathroom. At the cry SOLDIGNAC turns his head, but VATELIN who anticipates his intention, grabs his head in both his hands and turns it in the other direction.*)

SOLDIGNAC. What are you doing?
VATELIN. I beg your pardon, but my wife was not dressed.
SOLDIGNAC. I'm sorry – I didn't know. I'm glad you turned me away.
VATELIN. I agree. How would you like to go downstairs and play a game of billiards?
SOLDIGNAC. I'd like that very much. (*HE takes his hat.*)
VATELIN. Let's go, then.

(*There is a knock at the door.*)

Who is it this time?
REDILLON. (*enters with bag he had taken*) I beg your pardon, gentlemen.
VATELIN. Rédillon!
REDILLON. I took the wrong bag when I left here the last time. (*HE puts bag on chair near table.*)
VATELIN. Would you like to play billiards with Monsieur Soldignac? (*HE pushes him towards SOLDIGNAC.*)

REDILLON. We haven't met.
VATELIN. Monsieur Soldignac – Monsieur Rédillon. Why don't you two play a few games of billiards.
REDILLON. But I don't know how to play billiards.
VATELIN. That makes no difference. He'll show you.
REDILLON. I'm sorry, but I'm in a hurry. Some one is waiting for me. (*HE sits on sofa.*)
VATELIN. (*pulling him up*) Then don't sit down. It's not worth the trouble. We're leaving.
REDILLON. I see. But I have something to tell you.
VATELIN. Not now – we haven't time. Tell us another time. Where is my hat? (*HE goes to bed.*)

(*There is a knock at the door.*)

SOLDIGNAC. Come in!
CLARA. (*coming in*) Did Monsieur ring?
VATELIN. Yes – at least half an hour ago. I want you to take out this tray.
CLARA. Very well, monsieur. (*SHE takes out the tray.*)
REDILLON. Now, for my bag. I came to look for a bag.
VATELIN. (*handing REDILLON the bag he just brought in*) Here is your bag. Take it and go.
REDILLON. I don't want that one. I just brought that one back.
VATELIN. (*passing MARIA's bag to him*) Is it this one?
REDILLON. I don't know. Is this yours?
VATELIN. No.
REDILLON. Then it must be the one.

(*VATELIN puts PINCHARD's bag on table.*)

SOLDIGNAC. Let's go.

VATELIN. You go ahead. I'll join you in a moment.

(*REDILLON and SOLDIGNAC go out.*)

VATELIN. (*running to door right*) Quick! Maria!
MARIA. Can I come in? They go away?
VATELIN. Yes, but they're waiting for me. I have to play a game of billiards with your husband. Please don't leave this room. I'm going to lock you in, just to make sure. If anyone comes, hide in the bathroom, and don't come out until I return. Do you understand?
MARIA. Yes. Do you think I am imbecilly?
SOLDIGNAC. (*calling from outside*) Vatelin! Vatelin!
VATELIN. It's him. Hide!

(*SHE just has time to hide beside bed as SOLDIGNAC enters.*)

SOLDIGNAC. Well, Vatelin?
VATELIN. (*roughly pushing SOLDIGNAC out*) I'm coming! I'm coming! (*HE leaves and we hear him lock the door.*)
MARIA. Oh, I am scared. When I see my husband, my heart bounce on my teeth. I got to get hell out of here. Where is my close? (*SHE looks around for her clothes, then hears voices in hall.*) Someone coming. Caramba! I go hide. (*SHE goes into bathroom.*)
PINCHARD. (*outside*) Fine thing. The door is locked and I forgot to get a key. Boy – will you open the door for me?
VICTOR'S VOICE. Yes, monsieur.

(*The key turns in door, PINCHARD and WIFE come in.*)

PINCHARD. (*supporting his wife to help her walk*) It will pass, Coco. Sit down here. (*HE has her sit down.*) It's too bad this happened in the theatre. We should have left before it was over. (*sees his bag*) They brought my bag up. I knew I must have left it downstairs. (*HE looks at his suffering wife. The following phrases are completely without voice and should be seen by audience.*) Do-you-feel-better?

(*SHE shakes her head "no".*)

You're-still-sick?

(*SHE nods "yes".*)

Show-me-your-tongue.

(*SHE sticks out her tongue.*)

It-looks-all-right.

(*SHE makes a grimace.*)

You-ought-to-go-to-bed.

(*SHE nods agreement.*)

Good-night!

(*SHE comes to him and kisses him. Then PINCHARD speaks aloud.*)

Oh, yes, it's our anniversary. (*HE kisses her forehead.*)

Twenty-five years.

(*SHE goes in alcove, between bed and wall, starts to undress.*)

I'm going to prepare a sleeping potion for her. (*digs into bag*) Where is my pharmacy? (*pulls out his slippers*) My slippers! (*HE throws them down, then pulls out another pair*) Your slippers, Coco. (*HE takes them to her.*)
MADAME PINCHARD. (*behind the bed*) Thank you.
PINCHARD. (*pulling a light jacket from bag*) Coco, here's your jacket. (*hands it to her*) And here's my pharmacy. (*opening kit of drugs*)
MADAME PINCHARD. Give me my comb.
PINCHARD. (*taking it from bag, hands it to her over the bed*) Here it is. (*HE takes carafe, glass and spoon that are on nightstand and brings them to table. MADAME has taken off blouse and is in her skirt, her hair hanging down. SHE sits on bed and combs her hair. The bell under her rings, and keeps ringing. PINCHARD doesn't hear at first as HE sits at table to prepare his solution.*) One, two, three drops of laudanum. (*raises head*) Who is the idiot that's amusing himself ringing bells at this hour? (*back to his potion*) four, five, six drops. (*gets up*) That ringing is getting on my nerves. (*opens rear door and yells down the hall*) Aren't you about finished, bell ringer?
VOICE IN THE HALL. Who's ringing that bell?
PINCHARD. I don't know – but I've had my fill – in both ears. (*yelling*) Stop it! People want to sleep!
MADAME PINCHARD. (*rises to see what's going on, and the bell stops*) What's going on?
PINCHARD. It stopped. It was about time.

ACT II   THE FRENCH HAVE A WORD   89

VOICE IN THE HALL. It stopped. Thank you, Monsieur.

PINCHARD. Don't mention it. (*HE closes door.*)

MADAME PINCHARD. What were you doing?

PINCHARD. Nothing! Nothing! Go to bed. It's late. (*HE pushes her towards the bed.*) I'm going to bed too. I finally made that moron stop ringing. (*HE takes off his jacket, and MADAME gets into bed again, on wall side, starting the bell ringing.*) They're starting again. It's going to make me mad. (*Sitting on bed in order to take off his shoes and put on his slippers, HE activates the other bell which rings along with the first one.*) There's another one joining the party. There must be a convention of bell ringers in this hotel. I never heard such an ungodly racket. (*HE is taking off a boot, back to the door at left, from which comes LUCIENNE followed by PONTAGNAC.*)

LUCIENNE. It's you—you beast! (*SHE approaches PINCHARD from behind, grabs his shoulders and causes him to fall forward on the floor, with one boot still on.*) It's not Vatelin! Oh, my God! (*SHE runs back into room left with PONTAGNAC.*)

PINCHARD. (*getting up, one boot in his hand, and seeing no one, limps around in one boot, looking everywhere.*) Where did they go? I heard a voice. Who knocked me down?

VICTOR. (*entering*) What's going on, monsieur?

CLARA. (*who came in behind him*) Is that you ringing a bell?

PINCHARD. Me?

MANAGER. (*coming in, leaving door open*) You shouldn't ring like that. You'll wake up everyone in the hotel.

PINCHARD. Do you think I'm the one that's ringing?
A GUEST. (*in bathrobe over pajamas*) Haven't you finished playing with that bell? My wife can't sleep.
ANOTHER GUEST. (*wandering in*) Who's making all that racket? I've had enough of it.
PINCHARD. Who are all these people? Will you go away! Take off!
MANAGER. Yes, we will, when you stop ringing that bell.
ALL. Yes, stop it!
PINCHARD. Do I look like a Swiss bell-ringer? Do you see me ringing a bell? Do you see anyone ringing a bell? Is someone here ringing a bell?
MANAGER. It seems so, monsieur.
PINCHARD. Do you always come into a man's room like this in the middle of the night? Get the hell out of here — all of you.
ALL. Oh!
PINCHARD. (*near the bed, furious*) I said — the hell out! The — hell — out! (*To emphasize the last three words HE beats his fist on the mattress, and the bell responds with three short rings. HE stops, astonished, looks at the bed, hits the mattress three times again and again hears three short rings.*) What's going on here? (*HE sits on the bed, the bell rings until HE gets up.*) The bell is in this bed.
ALL. In the bed?
PINCHARD. It must be. (*HE pulls out the bell under the mattress on his side.*) That's a fine joke. I'd like to know the blithering idiot who amuses himself like that.
ALL. (*astonished*) Oh!
PINCHARD. There must be another one under my wife.

(*ALL except PINCHARD go to side of bed where MADAME is.*)

MADAME PINCHARD. (*frightened*) Who is it? What do you want of me? Pinchard, these men are after me.

PINCHARD. It's not you they want.

MANAGER. Don't be alarmed, madame. (*HE reaches under the mattress, causing MADAME to cringe.*) Ah, here is the other one.

PINCHARD. (*taking the bell*) What did I tell you? I'd like to know why these bells were put there.

MANAGER. I have no idea.

PINCHARD. If someone is trying to make fun of a respectable couple spending their twenty-fifth anniversary together in Paris, I feel sorry for him.

MANAGER. I assure you I understand none of this.

PINCHARD. Well, it's all over. Everyone can go now, and leave us in peace.

ALL. (*MANAGER, GUESTS, VICTOR, and CLARA form group by the door and say in lilting fashion, almost singing*) Happy anniversary!

PINCHARD. Forget it! We've already been to the Opera. Move out! On the double! (*They rush out and HE slams the door on them.*) This room was getting to be like an army barracks.

MADAME PINCHARD. (*on her knees in bed, a pillow in her arms*) What was it?

PINCHARD. You didn't hear a thing, did you, Coco? You're lucky.

MADAME PINCHARD. What did all those people want?

PINCHARD. Nothing, nothing.

MADAME PINCHARD. They frightened me. My pains were about to go away, but now they're starting again. (*SHE lies down again.*)

PINCHARD. You ought to have a hot poultice.

MADAME PINCHARD. How do you expect me to understand? You're in a bad light and I can't see what you are saying.

PINCHARD. (*takes candle from nightstand, holds it in front of him, speaking with lips*) You-ought-to-have-a-hot-poultice.

MADAME PINCHARD. I think so. But where are you going to find it?

PINCHARD. (*goes to ring bell for service, then opens his bag*) I have everything I need. I brought it just in case.

VICTOR. (*enters*) Did you ring, monsieur?

PINCHARD. Yes, this time I really rang. Would you have them heat these things in a little water, and make a poultice for my wife. She's suffering.

VICTOR. But there's no one in the kitchen at this hour.

PINCHARD. Well, is there a stove in the kitchen?

VICTOR. Oh, yes, monsieur Major – a gas stove.

PINCHARD. Then lead me to the kitchen and I'll make the poultice myself.

VICTOR. Very well, major. Will you permit me to help you with your jacket?

PINCHARD. (*who had picked up jacket and is struggling to get it on*) No, I won't permit you, I order you to. (*With VICTOR's help HE gets on his jacket.*) Soldier, if I ever run into you in an infirmary, I'm going to slap a poultice on you for twelve hours. (*turns to bed*) I'll be back in five minutes, Coco.

MADAME PINCHARD. What?

PINCHARD. (*without sound, holding candle to light his face*) I'll-be-back-in-five-minutes. I'm-going-to-make-a-poultice. (*HE leaves with VICTOR. The stage is silent a moment and then MARIA comes out of bathroom.*)

MARIA. I think the people gone now. But Cray-peen, he no come back. If I find my close, I go. Where did he put my close? (*SHE looks around, then notices*

MADAME PINCHARD *in bed.*) Caramba! There is somebodee een the bed! (*SHE runs, frightened, into bathroom. The stage is empty a moment we hear a key turning in lock of rear door, with someone pushing against door, then VATELIN enters.*)

VATELIN. That's strange! I could have sworn that I locked the door when I left. What a leech Soldignac is. I thought I would never get rid of him. Now to set Maria free. (*HE hears a snoring in the bed.*) She's already asleep. Nothing bothers her. (*Takes his bag from behind sofa, puts it on table and takes out a pair of slippers which HE puts by bed. Then HE places a chair by the bed for his clothes.*) It must be her Spanish nature. They like siestas. I'm not going to wake her up. I'll just slip into bed quietly and not disturb her restful sleep. That will make things much more restful for me, too. (*starts to undress, trips on PINCHARD's shoes and picks one up.*) What big feet Maria has. They must have big feet in Spain. (*HE takes off his shoes and places them by PINCHARD's.*) Good God, I'm thirsty. (*HE sees glass that PINCHARD had prepared on table.*) Oh, that's luck! (*HE drinks it down.*) That was good, but it tasted strange. (*HE finishes undressing down to his underwear. HE yawns.*) My eyes are getting heavy. I'm going to go to sleep without disturbing my mistress. And that's the way I like it. (*HE slides into bed.*) She takes up most of the bed, but I'm not going to move her. Oh, I forgot to take off my hat. (*HE throws hat on foot of bed.*) That will keep my feet warm. Oh, I've never been so sleepy. I wonder if Maria could have put some strychnine in that water. (*yawns and is quickly asleep*)

(*The door opens and VICTOR opens door to allow*

PINCHARD *with his poultice to come in, then leaves, closing door behind him.*)

PINCHARD. Are you there, Coco? It's hot, Coco. (*HE uncovers VATELIN with right hand and slaps the poultice on his stomach with the other hand.*)

VATELIN. Oh!

PINCHARD. Who is that?

VATELIN. Who goes there? A thief?

PINCHARD. There's a man in bed with my wife!

MADAME PINCHARD. (*waking up*) Who's there? Oh, my God, there's a man in the bed.

VATELIN. Who is this woman?

PINCHARD. (*grabbing him by the throat*) You low-life, what are you doing there?

VATELIN. Let go of me!

PINCHARD AND MADAME. Help! Help!

VATELIN. Let go of me!

PINCHARD. (*yelling*) There's a man in my wife's bed!

LUCIENNE. (*coming in with PONTAGNAC*) It's you — miserable cheat!

VATELIN. Oh, God! My wife! (*HE pushes PINCHARD away, grabs his clothes, chair and all, and runs out the rear door.*)

PINCHARD. (*to LUCIENNE*) You're a witness! He was trying to rape my wife.

LUCIENNE. I saw him very well, monsieur.

PINCHARD. Catch him! He was in bed with Coco! (*HE runs out, in hot pursuit.*)

MADAME PINCHARD. (*During the past few minutes SHE has got out of bed, put on her skirt and slippers.*) My husband! Pinchard! Where did he go? (*SHE runs out after him.*)

PONTAGNAC. (*to LUCIENNE*) Well, are you convinced?

LUCIENNE. Oh, yes! The traitor!

PONTAGNAC. Did I do right to insist that you stay here?

LUCIENNE. Oh, yes, you were right. My mind is made up now.

PONTAGNAC. I hope you will know how to avenge yourself, as you said you would.

LUCIENNE. Oh, yes, I swear to you. I shall keep my word.

PONTAGNAC. Bravo!

LUCIENNE. I said I would take a lover – well, I take that lover!

PONTAGNAC. I am the happiest of men.

LUCIENNE. And if my husband asks you the name of my lover, I want you to tell him.

PONTAGNAC. There's no need of that.

LUCIENNE. Oh, yes. Tell him my lover is his best friend, Ernest Rédillon.

PONTAGNAC. (*suffocating*) Huh! Red –

LUCIENNE. Good-bye, I am going now for my vengeance. (*SHE dashes out quickly at left, locking door behind her.*)

PONTAGNAC. Lucienne, in the name of God – Lucienne. (*HE rushes to left door but finds it is locked.*) Locked! (*HE runs to rear door but bumps into Police Inspector DUVAL who is entering, followed by a GENDARME, and SOLDIGNAC.*)

DUVAL. Stop! In the name of the law!

PONTAGNAC. Police!

SOLDIGNAC. (*holding billiard cue*) Ah, here is her

"love." (*HE puts down the billiard cue by fireplace, takes off his coat and practices some karate movements by the wall.*)

DUVAL. We know everything, monsieur. You are here with Monsieur Soldignac's wife.

PONTAGNAC. Me?

DUVAL. Where is your accomplice hiding?

PONTAGNAC. My accomplice?

DUVAL. Find her, Pierre! (*The GENDARME goes toward bathroom door.*) Your name, monsieur?

PONTAGNAC. Pontagnac.

GENDARME. (*coming in with MARIA*) Here's the woman, sir.

PONTAGNAC. Who is that?

MARIA. (*seeing SOLDIGNAC*) Mi marido!

SOLDIGNAC. Good God! My wife!

(*SOLDIGNAC and MARIA, who is still restrained by Gendarme, dispute in Spanish, ad lib, almost at the same time:*

SOLDIGNAC – Qué haces aquí?	MARIA – A ti que te importa?
SOLDIGNAC – Me engañas!	MARIA – Mentiras. Eres tu!
SOLDIGNAC – No es verdad!	MARIA – Sí, Sí!
SOLDIGNAC – Puta!	MARIA – Maricón!
SOLDIGNAC – Cochina!	MARIA – Roñoso!

INSPECTOR DUPONT. (*entering with MADAME PONTAGNAC*) In the name of the law! Monsieur Pontagnac, we have a complaint against you.

PONTAGNAC. Another one! (*sees MADAME PONTAGNAC*) My wife!
MADAME PONTAGNAC. Do your duty, Inspector Dupont. (*SHE leaves, and PONTAGNAC tries to follow her, but DUPONT restrains him.*)
PONTAGNAC. Yvonne! Wait!
DUPONT. Don't make matters worse for you, monsieur.
SOLDIGNAC. (*seizing PONTAGNAC away from DUPONT*) It's the two of us now! (*HE starts raining karate blows on PONTAGNAC, while MARIA beats on both inspectors to keep them away.*)
REDILLON. (*enters with Maria's bag*) What's going on?

(*The two inspectors approach him.*)

DUPONT. Who are you?
REDILLON. I beg your pardon – I got the wrong bag. (*Changes the bag with VATELIN's which is on the table and quickly ducks out. The fight goes on.*)

END OF ACT TWO

ACT THREE

THE FRENCH HAVE A WORD FOR IT

SCENE: *The den in REDILLON's apartment. It resembles a room in a harem. At left is door leading to bedroom, at right a door to another room. At right there is a lavish divan with a backing of Middle-Eastern fabrics. There is a chair near the divan. At left rear are double doors that open on a hallway which leads to the outside and to other parts of the house. Directly across the hall can be seen another room which has a table, chairs. A long window is at right of the room. A fireplace is at left. A table is at L of center. It is a low table of oriental design. Two poufs and stacks of cushions are near it.*

AT RISE: *JEROME, an old servant and friend of the family, enters rear, holding ARMANDINE's skirt on his arm. He is a free spirit, not resembling a valet, and his manner of dress is casual, a beret, and striped sweater.*

JEROME. Another skirt! Always skirts. He's incorrigible. But what can you do with today's young people? They burn their candles at both ends and the flame never goes out. They're always on the run. But I don't run. I'm not interested in the new movement. I like myself as I am. Why not? It's too late to change anything. (*knocks on door left*)

REDILLON'S VOICE. Who is it? As if I didn't know.

JEROME. It's Jerome, your faithful watchdog.

REDILLON. (*thrusting out his head*) What do you want, bane of my life – a bone?

JEROME. I wish to inform you that it is eleven o'clock.

REDILLON. Well! So it's eleven o'clock! In one hour it will be noon. Go away! (*HE slams door, almost hitting JEROME on nose.*)

JEROME. Imagine! A child I saw being born. Respect has gone out the window. And his father – my own milk brother – made me promise to take care of him. (*looks at portrait on wall, or glances at a picture on table, or can simply lift his eyes toward the balcony*) Old friend, wherever you are, how do you expect me to take care of him when he's busy taking care of all the women in Paris? Does he ever listen to me? You know as well as I do that he doesn't give a damn what I say. Telling him to look after his life is like telling the Prince of Monaco to look after Africa. But I'm the one elected to be valet to all the girls he brings here. I have pressed more skirts than the biggest laundry in Paris. Old friend – (*HE kisses his imaginary friend on both cheeks.*) You are lucky to be where you are. (*HE hears voices in REDILLON's room, goes to left and listens.*) Perhaps they've decided to change the routine.

(*ARMANDINE, wrapped in a long man's robe, hair hanging down, comes in followed by REDILLON who allows JEROME to pass into bedroom with the skirt, gaving him a pat on the head.*)

ARMANDINE. (*going to fireplace, SHE almost trips on the long robe.*) This robe is too long.

REDILLON. It's too long for you, but not for me.

ARMANDINE. (*running hands through her hair*) But it happens to be draped around my gorgeous body. But let's talk about my handbag. Did you have to bring every bag in the hotel—one after the other—except mine?

REDILLON. How did I know what yours looked like?

ARMANDINE. It seems you could have accidently brought mine—just once. (*SHE leaves the fireplace.*)

REDILLON. (*an enormous yawn*) Oh . . . . !

ARMANDINE. What is it, old man?

REDILLON. What?

ARMANDINE. Are you feeling run-down?

REDILLON. I'm tired, that's all.

ARMANDINE. (*sitting near table*) After being in bed for eleven hours?

(*JEROME comes in with duster, looking at REDILLON with pity.*)

REDILLON. In bed? That's the trouble. What I need is four hours of sleep.

JEROME. Why do you get yourself into such a state?

REDILLON. (*wearily*) What do you want, Jerome?

JEROME. Nothing.

REDILLON. Then why do you have to stand there and look at me?

JEROME. Oh, Ernest, you're wearing yourself out. Destroying yourself.

ARMANDINE. Huh?

REDILLON. What?

JEROME. I'm worried about you.

REDILLON. Oh, leave me alone. Who asked you anything?

JEROME. You don't have to ask me—I just tell you. I'm worried about you. (*HE goes out at rear.*)

REDILLON. Have you ever seen anything like that? You'll have to excuse him—he's an old servant of the family.

ARMANDINE. (*on armchair*) He's very familiar.

REDILLON. He's like a member of the family. He's my milk uncle.

ARMANDINE. Your milk uncle? What's that?

REDILLON. That's one way of saying it. His mother nursed my father while she was nursing him. So we're milk relatives.

ARMANDINE. That's all right, but it sounds strange for him to speak to you as he does.

REDILLON. What do you expect? He saw me being born. I didn't see him. (*yawns*) I have never been so tired. (*HE stretches on divan, face to audience.*)

ARMANDINE. Oh, Ernest, you're never going to break any records.

REDILLON. I've never wanted to be the champion of France.

ARMANDINE. (*her knee on the divan between REDILLON's legs*) You do well enough. (*SHE kisses him.*) I think I bore you when I kiss you.

REDILLON. (*without conviction*) Oh, no.

ARMANDINE. Yes, I already bore you.

REDILLON. Not at all. (*imploring*) But rest a bit!

ARMANDINE. Men are like that. They treat you wonderfully at night, but the morning after, they want to chase you away. (*SHE gets up.*)

REDILLON. Not until the day after tomorrow. Kiss me.

(SHE *kisses him in a long kiss as* JEROME *comes in, rear, bringing a glass of wine on a tray.* HE *interrupts the kiss with a blast.*)

JEROME. Is there no end to this debauchery? (*HE places himself between* REDILLON *and* ARMANDINE.) Please, mademoiselle, have pity on him. Haven't you had enough of him?

ARMANDINE. (*going left*) What's wrong with him? (*SHE sits at table.*)

JEROME. Just look at him. He has no blood. He's a zombie.

REDILLON. Jerome, do you know that I'm going to throw you out of here?

JEROME. Do your worst – I won't leave. Here – drink this!

REDILLON. No!

JEROME. Drink it, I say. I'm losing my patience.

REDILLON. All right – I'll drink it, obstinate mule. (*HE takes the glass.*)

ARMANDINE. What is that?

JEROME. It's medicinal herb wine.

ARMANDINE. What for?

JEROME. What for? To restore some of the vital juices that *you* have drained out of him.

ARMANDINE. Me?

JEROME. (*pulling her to one side, speaks in low voice.*) For God's sake – remember he is only a child. He's only thirty-two. He's not like me.

REDILLON. (*sitting on sofa and drinking*) What are you whispering to her?

JEROME. Nothing, nothing! Mind your own business! (*admiring* ARMANDINE's *cleavage at close range*)

ARMANDINE. (*mockingly to REDILLON while acting kittenish with JEROME*) We have some deep secrets between us.

JEROME. (*enjoying the close contact, to REDILLON*) They don't concern you.

REDILLON. I beg your pardon. (*holds out the empty glass which JEROME takes*) Did anyone come to see me today?

JEROME. Yes. First there was Pluplu.

ARMANDINE. Did Pluplu come here? (*SHE sits near them in order to hear everything.*)

JEROME. Yes, she wanted to see you. Of course you know what she wanted.

REDILLON. What did you tell her?

JEROME. I told her that you were at your mother's. She wanted to wait, but I told her you usually stay three or four days when you visit your mother.

ARMANDINE. You did right. I wouldn't have wanted to meet her face to face. (*SHE rises.*)

JEROME. And Monsieur Brie was here.

ARMANDINE. (*Her back to audience, SHE hits on the table.*) Brie! Brie! I know that name.

REDILLON. No, you don't know him. He's past the age.

ARMANDINE. Oh!

REDILLON. He's an antique dealer who lives in this building. Sometimes, when he has something unusual, he drops by.

ARMANDINE. I remember now. I was thinking of Monsieur Roquefort. I haven't seen him for some time. But I was positive I knew someone who sounded like cheese. (*SHE passes between table and fireplace.*)

REDILLON. Jerome, what did Monsieur Roquefort want — I mean Monsieur Brie? (*to ARMANDINE*) You're mixing me up with all your cheeses.

JEROME. He said he had a rare chastity belt from the fourteenth.

REDILLON. Oh.

ARMANDINE. The fourteenth what?

JEROME. The fourteenth over-sexed female like you that wore it.

ARMANDINE. But I've never worn one. They never have my size.

REDILLON. Oh, he means it's from the fourteenth century. What else did the man have?

JEROME. That's all.

(*A ring is heard.*)

Someone is here.

REDILLON. If it's a woman, I'm not in.

JEROME. You didn't have to tell me that. (*HE goes out rear.*)

ARMANDINE. No we're not here! It might be Pluplu, and there would probably be a fight. I don't like dumb blondes. (*SHE goes toward bedroom door.*)

REDILLON. Where are you going?

ARMANDINE. I'm going to dress. If it's a woman, I'm going to bounce out of here.

JEROME'S VOICE IN HALL. No, Madame, he is not here, I assure you. (*HE sticks his head in the room.*) It's one of those! Get the hell out of here!

REDILLON. Let's get out! (*HE goes into door L with ARMANDINE.*)

JEROME. Come in, madame, see for yourself if you don't believe me.

LUCIENNE. No one.

JEROME. I repeat that he is *not* here.

LUCIENNE. Just the same, you go tell him that Madame Vatelin wants to speak to him.

JEROME. Madame Vatelin! The wife of his friend Vatelin whom he visits so often?

LUCIENNE. Exactly right.

JEROME. That's quite different. Please excuse me. I mistook you for a woman of easy virtue.

LUCIENNE. Well! Thank you so much!

JEROME. It was meant as a compliment. (*calling into bedroom door*) Ernest! It's Madame Vatelin.

REDILLON'S VOICE. What did you say?

JEROME. It's Madame Vatelin. Don't you know who Madame Vatelin is? (*to LUCIENNE*) Here he is.

REDILLON. (*entering*) Is it possible? You? In my house? Why? (*HE invites her to sit down.*)

LUCIENNE. (*sitting near table*) Does it really astonish you? Well, it astonishes me.

REDILLON. (*goes to JEROME, speaks low*) Tell the person in there that I must excuse myself because of some important business. Tell her whatever you want, but when she finishes dressing, steer her out of here.

JEROME. Plan understood. Will execute. (*HE knocks at door left.*)

VOICE OF ARMANDINE. Don't come in.

JEROME. Don't worry about it. (*HE goes in the door.*)

REDILLON. So you're really here?

LUCIENNE. You know about last night, don't you?

REDILLON. No.

LUCIENNE. Well, since I'm here, you must have guessed that something happened.

REDILLON. What!

LUCIENNE. I surprised my husband in a hotel room — flagrante delicto.

REDILLON. No! And you've come to make love to me?
LUCIENNE. I always keep my word.
REDILLON. *(taking her hands and having her sit on divan)* Oh, Lucienne, how happy I am. Take me, use me. I'm yours.
LUCIENNE. But I came here to say that to you.
REDILLON. Does it matter which of us says it?
JEROME. *(appears at door, left)* Psst!
REDILLON. What? *(JEROME makes sign that ARMANDINE is going to leave.)* Good!
LUCIENNE. What's going on?
REDILLON. Somone wants to pass. Hide behind me. There's no need for you to be seen.

(LUCIENNE rises, stands back-to-back with REDILLON who is facing rear. ARMANDINE comes out, dressed waves at him. HE waves back, and SHE leaves at rear with JEROME.)

LUCIENNE. Well?
REDILLON. Just a moment.

(JEROME reappears, makes sign by sliding one hand off the back of his other hand to indicate SHE has gone.)

Yes? Good.

(JEROME points at LUCIENNE and waves a warning finger, then leaves.)

They're gone, Lucienne.
LUCIENNE. Ah!

ACT III   THE FRENCH HAVE A WORD   107

(*THEY quit their back-to-back position.*)

REDILLON. Sit down.

LUCIENNE. Can you believe it of that miserable wretch?

REDILLON. Who?

LUCIENNE. Who? My husband, of course.

REDILLON. (*sitting beside her*) Oh, yes. I wasn't thinking.

LUCIENNE. What a faithful wife I've been to him. I even repulsed the advances of poor Rédillon.

REDILLON. Yes, poor old Rédillon, who has waited so long.

LUCIENNE. But now I'll love him far more than I ever repulsed him. I will belong to him body and soul. That will be my vengeance.

REDILLON. Oh, Lucienne, Lucienne. (*HE is almost asleep. His head nods, and HE wakes up only when JEROME thrusts his head in the rear door and speaks.*)

JEROME. (*HE is wearing a beret.*) I'm going out to get some cutlets.

REDILLON. (*roughly*) Do you have to come in here to talk about cutlets? (*realizing LUCIENNE is there*) Oh, Lucienne, Lucienne. (*gets up and runs to hall, and calls after JEROME*) And get some green beans for a change.

JEROME'S VOICE. I'll look for some.

REDILLON. (*coming back down*) He has a mania for serving potatoes every day. I'm getting saturated. (*sitting*) Please excuse me, but he's an old servant of the family, and he's a little – uh – well, he lives very close to the ground. He doesn't swim in the ideal as we do. (*HE rests his head and is almost asleep again.*)

LUCIENNE. (*rising and going left*) So you think that I'm ready to swim in the ideal? (*SHE comes between table and fireplace.*)

REDILLON. (*shaking his head to wake up*) Huh? What was I just saying?

LUCIENNE. You were saying that your servant has a mania for making you eat potatoes.

REDILLON. No—before that.

LUCIENNE. You were saying: "Oh, Lucienne, Lucienne"

REDILLON. (*lyrically, trying to regain his composure*) Oh, Lucienne. (*coming to her*) Lucienne, Lucienne. (*leads her to the divan*) Tell me that I'm not in a dream. Are you really mine? Mine alone?

LUCIENNE. (*seated*) Yes—yours alone.

REDILLON. How happy I am.

LUCIENNE. I'm glad. It's nature's way of compensation. The misfortune of one often brings happiness to another.

REDILLON. Oh, yes, Lucienne. Please put your head on my shoulder.

LUCIENNE. (*SHE starts to do so, but is conscious of her hat.*) Wait—this hat bothers me. (*SHE takes it off.*)

REDILLON. Give it to me. (*SHE does. HE holds it in one hand while the other slips around her waist.*) Oh, the fragrance of your hair makes me drunk. You smell like a garden of flowers. And all mine! Oh, what bouquets I am going to pick. (*HE leans back and his eyes close, one hand extended, holding her hat.*)

LUCIENNE. Are you going to keep holding my hat like that?

REDILLON. (*Shaking himself awake, the hat falls but HE picks it up quickly.*) No—wait. (*HE puts the hat on table and comes back to LUCIENNE. HE kisses her.*) It's the first time I've been able to caress your skin with my lips.

LUCIENNE. That's it! Vengeance! Vengeance!
REDILLON. Oh, yes.
LUCIENNE. From today on, I am no longer the wife of Vatelin, I am your wife—and you will marry me.
REDILLON. Oh, yes, yes.
LUCIENNE. (*speaking to the rear as if her husband were there*) A man I loved—a man to whom I gave everything! My love, my fidelity, my innocent virginity.
REDILLON. (*awakened by her tirade*) Don't talk about your husband now. I don't want his image to be always between us. Oh, my Lucienne. (*HE gets on his knees facing her.*)
JEROME. (*thrusting his head in at rear*) I'm back!
REDILLON. Don't come in!
JEROME. What on earth are you doing down there on your knees?
REDILLON. Do I have to account to you? Get out of here!
JEROME. If you insist.
REDILLON. And close the door!
JEROME. Why? Are you cold?
REDILLON. Because I told you to. And don't come in unless I call you.
JEROME. I couldn't find any green beans.
REDILLON. I don't give a damn!
JEROME. So I got some potatoes. We haven't had potatoes since yesterday. (*HE goes out, closing the door.*)
REDILLON. Please excuse him. He's an old servant of the family, but you would never know it. Now—where were we? (*back on his knees*) Oh, Lucienne, let me press you to my body.
LUCIENNE. Do you love me?
REDILLON. Do I love you! But I'm not close enough

to you. Make a little space for me next to you. (*HE sits on edge, but facing in opposite direction.*) That's better. Now I can press you to my heart.

LUCIENNE. Then the fortune teller's prediction will come true.

REDILLON. (*eyes half-closed*) What prediction?

LUCIENNE. That I would have two romantic adventures in my life – one at twenty-five, and one at fifty-eight. The first is being fulfilled. I'm twenty-five – or close enough.

REDILLON. Yes, and I'm the hero. (*hugging her*) Wait – not like this. (*HE extends body full length on floor, his feet to rear, his face towards audience.*)

LUCIENNE. What are you doing?

REDILLON. I feel better this way, and I can see you better. Kiss me!

(*SHE leans over, and HE pulls her down beside him to complete the kiss.*)

LUCIENNE. (*sitting up*) My dear!

(*REDILLON is about to go sound asleep on the floor.*)

Well? (*SHE taps him with her foot.*) Are you alive?

(*HE shudders as HE wakes up.*)

Well, don't you have anything more to say?

REDILLON. Oh, Lucienne, Lucienne. (*HE crawls over, puts his head on her lap, facing audience, and once more is almost asleep.*)

LUCIENNE. Lucienne, Lucienne! Is that all you know how to say? (*SHE gets up, and REDILLON falls to the floor.*) Is that all you know how to say?

REDILLON. (*sitting up*) Lucienne, I don't know if it's emotion or nerves, but I swear this is the first time this has happened to me.

LUCIENNE. And here's a man who always came to speak of his love.

REDILLON. (*rising*) But I love you. But please understand – I was so far from attaining my hopes – and now, all of a sudden – joy, love, passion – it baffles my reason. My head is turning.

LUCIENNE. I think it is.

REDILLON. And then there's the matter of scruples – scruples of an honorable man – which won't last long, but which have to be considered. I think about your husband, my good friend. To play an ugly trick on him is just too much. Let me have time to prepare for the new turn of events.

LUCIENNE. Your scruples are showing up rather late, my friend.

REDILLON. They will pass, I told you, but give me time to reflect. Come tomorrow, or this evening.

LUCIENNE. Tomorrow! This evening! But it's impossible. My husband will be here very soon.

REDILLON. What?

LUCIENNE. Yes! And when he arrives, I want my vengeance to be consummated – I want him to know that I have already been –

REDILLON. I understand. But your husband – here?

LUCIENNE. Yes. Yes. I sent him a letter saying: "You have deceived me, and now I deceive you in turn. If you doubt it, come to the home of your friend Rédillon. (*reaction from REDILLON*) "You will find me in the arms of my lover."

REDILLON. But that's madness. We were about to make a big blunder. It's strange, but I had the intuition. Something stronger than I am made me be reasonable.
VOICE OF JEROME. No, Madame, no!
VOICE OF MADAME PONTAGNAC. But I say "yes"!
REDILLON. Who is that?
MADAME PONTAGNAC. (*pushing in*) Get away from me!
REDILLON, LUCIENNE. Madame Pontagnac!
MADAME PONTAGNAC. Yes, it is. You weren't expecting to see me so soon, were you, Monsieur Redillon? Yesterday I told you that when I have proof that my husband is unfaithful, I would come to you and say: "I am yours – avenge me!"
LUCIENNE. What!
MADAME PONTAGNAC. (*taking off jacket and putting it on divan*) Well, monsieur, here I am. Avenge me! I am all yours.
REDILLON. You too?
LUCIENNE. What did you say?
REDILLON. (*aside, going upstage*) This is getting ridiculous.
LUCIENNE. Excuse me, Madame Pontagnac, but I think you are a bit too free with your "avenge me, I am all yours."
MADAME PONTAGNAC. Not at all. I had a business agreement with Monsieur Rédillon.
LUCIENNE. That's entirely possible, but allow me to say that I was here first.
MADAME PONTAGNAC. Perhaps so, but I wish to point out that I retained Monsieur Rédillon's services yesterday.
LUCIENNE. That's exactly what I did.
MADAME PONTAGNAC. Madame!
LUCIENNE. Madame!

ACT III THE FRENCH HAVE A WORD 113

REDILLON. (*coming between them*) In the name of Beelzebub, don't I have anything to say in this matter?

LUCIENNE. Yes—as the contractor you have a right to speak.

MADAME PONTAGNAC. Yes, speak.

REDILLON. Thank you. I most certainly will speak. This is all very astonishing, to say the least. You want to revenge yourselves on your respective husbands. So where do I fit in? Do you take me for a booby in the department of marital reprisals? (*HE looks at them as they stand there longingly.*) Yes, I think you do.

LUCIENNE. Well, which of the two will you take?

MADAME PONTAGNAC. Yes, which of the two?

REDILLON. Which of the two? You are both beautiful women, therefore I could scarcely choose one over the other. But if I choose both of you, I'm sure I should be dead before dinner time. So I say—neither of you—neither the one nor the other. That is the judgment of Solomon Ernest Rédillon.

THE TWO WOMEN. Oh, no!

REDILLON. Good-bye, my angels. (*HE moves away.*)

THE TWO WOMEN. Oh!

JEROME. (*thrusting in his head quickly at rear door*) It's Pluplu. She came back. She wants to speak to you.

REDILLON. Oh, no—I'm not receiving, and I'm not—(*shakes his head wearily*) Tell her that I'm dead, or that I shall be very soon.

JEROME. Very well. (*HE goes out.*)

LUCIENNE. Rédillon!

MADAME PONTAGNAC. Monsieur Rédillon!

REDILLON. No! I say, no! There's just so much that one man can deliver. I'm not a fountain that dispenses love and affection like Perrier water. (*HE rushes into room L and locks door. The* WOMEN *run to the door and pound on it but* HE *doesn't answer.*)

MADAME PONTAGNAC. I'm disgusted.

LUCIENNE. I too.

MADAME PONTAGNAC. You see what you have caused.

LUCIENNE. I think the fault is with you.

MADAME PONTAGNAC. My fault? You understand of course that this business is already very distressing to me.

LUCIENNE. Do you think I am here for pleasure?

MADAME PONTAGNAC. I was simply propelled by the idea of getting revenge.

LUCIENNE. I too.

MADAME PONTAGNAC. Can't you say anything but "I too"?

LUCIENNE. What else shall I say? Our situations are exactly the same.

MADAME PONTAGNAC. This is no way to force compromises from our husbands.

LUCIENNE. It's not fair to honest women.

JEROME. (*coming in at rear*) There is a young man here who is asking for Madame Vatelin.

LUCIENNE. Who is asking for me? A young man?

JEROME. Monsieur Pontagnac.

MADAME PONTAGNAC. My husband. Do you call him a young man?

JEROME. To me, he's young. I was already an adult when he was still wearing diapers.

MADAME PONTAGNAC. I wonder what he wants.

LUCIENNE. I don't know. But he's asking for me. He's just in time. I need someone to avenge me.

MADAME PONTAGNAC. What? You want—

LUCIENNE. Don't be alarmed—it's only in order to give a jolt to my husband.

ACT III   THE FRENCH HAVE A WORD   115

MADAME PONTAGNAC. Oh!

LUCIENNE. Will you let me use your husband? There will be no wear or tear.

MADAME PONTAGNAC. My pleasure. This will give me one more grievance against him.

LUCIENNE. Good. (*takes Yvonne's clothes and gives them to her*) Go in there, Madame. (*SHE indicates a door right, and MADAME goes in.*) Let Monsieur Pontagnac come in.

JEROME. Yes, Madame. (*HE introduces PONTAGNAC and leaves.*)

PONTAGNAC. Alone! Where is Rédillon?

LUCIENNE. I'm waiting for him.

PONTAGNAC. God be praised. I arrived in time. (*puts his hat on table*)

LUCIENNE. Why are you pursuing me? What do you want?

PONTAGNAC. What do I want? I want to prevent you from doing something foolish. I want to put myself between you and Rédillon — to snatch you from him.

LUCIENNE. By what right?

PONTAGNAC. What right? By the right of all the hornets' nests that fell on me last night, and all because I was trying to help you catch your husband. I have two criminal charges on my back — arrested by a husband I don't know, for being with a woman I don't know. Caught by my wife with this same woman that I don't know. A divorce for me is in prospect, and another divorce for the woman I don't know from the man I don't know, and in which I am named as accessory. And there is a rupture with my wife. The woman that I don't know, came this morning and told me in Spanish accent that I owe her reparation because of a brawl with the man I don't know. Add to all that, the scandal, the worry, and the criminal charges. And all of that did nothing but throw you into another man's arms. He reaps the harvest while I am the turkey.

LUCIENNE. Now let me tell you something. When you arrived just now, I thought to myself: "After all, it was Pontagnac who helped me to prove my husband's infidelity."

PONTAGNAC. Absolutely.

LUCIENNE. If anyone should avenge me, it's you.

PONTAGNAC. No! Is it possible?

LUCIENNE. If I ask you—?

PONTAGNAC. If you ask me, I'll be the happiest man in the world.

LUCIENNE. Then be the happiest of men. You are going to be my avenger. (*SHE takes off a garment that hides a velvet blouse, very low cut, no sleeves and attached to her shoulders with glittering stones. SHE unrolls her hair and shakes it to make it fall.*) My husband liked me like this. Do you think I am beautiful like this?

PONTAGNAC. Like the Princess of Bagdad.

LUCIENNE. Do you love me?

PONTAGNAC. All my life. (*HE goes quickly and locks the rear door.*)

LUCIENNE. Perfect! Sit down.

PONTAGNAC. Sit down? But I thought—

LUCIENNE. You thought right. But I must choose the moment when I am most desired. The man who loves me must be a slave who bends to my caprices. I said "sit down". (*sharply*) Sit down!

PONTAGNAC. Yes. (*HE sits near table.*) I obey you.

LUCIENNE. Take off your jacket.

PONTAGNAC. Beg pardon?

LUCIENNE. Take off your jacket – it reminds me of my husband.

PONTAGNAC. But I don't have on a shirt – only a false front.

LUCIENNE. That makes no difference. Reveal your falseness. (*SHE sits on divan.*)

PONTAGNAC. As you wish. (*HE takes off his jacket.*) What next?

LUCIENNE. Sit near me.

PONTAGNAC. (*sitting*) Here I am.

LUCIENNE. Take off your vest. You look silly in it.

PONTAGNAC. I'd rather keep it on, but I'll take it off, since you request it. (*HE removes the vest, leaving only the false shirt front, collar and tie.*) Don't I look ridiculous like this?

LUCIENNE. No more ridiculous than before. Don't let it distress you. (*SHE unbuttons one side of his suspenders in front.*) Who does your hair? You look like a waiter. (*SHE messes up his hair with vigorous movements.*) Now you look like an artist. (*SHE unbuttons the other side of his suspenders.*) Turn around!

(*HE turns around and SHE pulls his suspenders down so they drag behind him.*)

PONTAGNAC. (*turns to her, wants to embrace her*) Oh, Lucienne.

LUCIENNE. (*giving him a thump*) This is not the moment. When the moment arrives, you will know in a flash.

PONTAGNAC. I'm not made of wood you know.

LUCIENNE. Enough of that.

PONTAGNAC. All right.

(*LUCIENNE rises, takes newspaper from table, then sits again and reads the paper.*)

This is a strange way to make love!
LUCIENNE. (*over the newspaper*) There's a new play at the Palais-Royal.
PONTAGNAC. So?
LUCIENNE. Aren't you going?
PONTAGNAC. No!
LUCIENNE. Oh! (*SHE begins to read again. PONTAGNAC, not knowing what to do, starts to whistle through his teeth, looks around aimlessly, gets up, strolls around, hands behind back, looking at things in the room.*)
LUCIENNE. (*still holding the newspaper*) Sit down!
PONTAGNAC. (*sitting quickly*) Do I have to beg for a lump of sugar like a poodle?
LUCIENNE. Be patient.
PONTAGNAC. But what are we waiting for?
LUCIENNE. For that special moment when my vengeance will cry out to the sky, and will be known to the world.
PONTAGNAC. What are you talking about?
LUCIENNE. Quiet! I think I hear someone.
PONTAGNAC. I don't hear anyone.
LUCIENNE. But I'm sure that someone is here. Perhaps it is my husband.

(*PONTAGNAC rises and moves about nervously.*)

PONTAGNAC. What did you say?
LUCIENNE. Perhaps it is my husband.
PONTAGNAC. Your husband?
LUCIENNE. Now my vengeance will be complete.

VOICE OUTSIDE (DUPONT). In the name of the law, open the door.

PONTAGNAC. It's them! Hide yourself.

LUCIENNE. Hide? Don't you love me enough to have a dispute with my husband?

PONTAGNAC. Of course.

VOICE (POLICEMAN). Open the door!

LUCIENNE. This is the way I want it. Before the whole world. Pontagnac, I am yours.

PONTAGNAC. What? Now?

LUCIENNE. Now or never!

PONTAGNAC. (*drawing away*) Oh, no – not like this.

VOICE (DUVAL). Open or I'll break the door down.

PONTAGNAC. I'll open the door. (*As HE goes, LUCIENNE falls on divan and assumes the most sultry, indecent pose SHE can think of, while SHE looks defiantly in direction where her husband should be coming in.*)

VATELIN. (*entering with INSPECTORS DUVAL and DUPONT and POLICEMAN followed by JEROME*) Oh, that indecent Jezebel!

DUVAL. No one will move!

PONTAGNAC. But, inspector, I –

DUPONT. You again? How you do get around. Do you have a bicycle?

PONTAGNAC. But, monsieur, I don't understand. I was paying a visit to Madame.

DUPONT. In that get-up? Dress yourself, monsieur.

(*PONTAGNAC dresses but forgets to fasten suspenders, leaving them hanging behind him.*)

REDILLON. (*coming out of his room*) What the devil is going on here?

DUVAL. (*to LUCIENNE*) Madame, I am the Police Inspector of your area, and I have come at the request of Monsieur Vatelin, your husband.

LUCIENNE. Very well, monsieur. No need to read me the law. Monsieur Pontagnac will tell you things in order to save my reputation. It's his duty as a gentleman, but I want the truth to be known by all. I came here of my own free will and pleasure, and if I came it was to find Monsieur Pontagnac, my lover.

VATELIN. She admits it!

LUCIENNE. I authorize you to register a complaint against me.

VATELIN. (*falls in chair*) Oh!

MADAME PONTAGNAC. (*appearing at door right*) It's my turn now.

PONTAGNAC. My wife!

MADAME PONTAGNAC. Please understand, Inspector, that I, Yvonne Pontagnac, wife of Pontagnac, came to this house to meet my lover.

PONTAGNAC. What did you say?

MADAME PONTAGNAC. Adieu, monsieur. (*SHE leaves at rear, PONTAGNAC runs after her but DUPONT grabs his suspenders that are trailing and holds him back.*)

DUPONT. Please, Monsieur, we will have need of you.

PONTAGNAC. You heard what she said. She has a lover. Where is he? I want to kill him. Let him show himself if he's not a miserable coward.

JEROME. (*advancing, with exaggerated bravado, left hand on waist*) I – am – the – man.

PONTAGNAC. You?

JEROME. I am your wife's lover!

REDILLON. (*to JEROME*) What are you saying?

JEROME. (*low to REDILLON*) Shut up! I'm saving you! (*aloud to PONTAGNAC*) I repeat—I am the lover!

PONTAGNAC. We shall see each other again. Give me your card.

JEROME. I have no card, but you can find me here. I am Jerome, personal valet to Ernest. (*HE taps REDILLON fondly on the cheek as HE steps back.*) My little Ernest.

PONTAGNAC. My God! A servant! How low can she sink?

(*DUVAL and DUPONT converse privately a moment.*)

DUPONT. Don't you see that you are being made a fool of? Don't you see that this is the work of an angry woman, and not an unfaithful wife?

PONTAGNAC. I'll find out.

DUVAL. Meanwhile we have need of some writing material. We must make a report.

REDILLON. In there, Inspectors. (*Indicates rear door. JEROME opens it and the others follow him into room across the hall. DUPONT still holds PONTAGNAC by his suspenders. The INSPECTORS sit at the table in the room across the hall. JEROME goes out of sight. Only VATELIN and REDILLON remain in the room. REDILLON goes downstage.*) Well, this is a fine hash. (*goes close to VATELIN who is seated in chair, head in hands*) Come now, Vatelin, my good friend.

VATELIN. But you don't know how painful this is. It's like ping-ping-ping—right here. (*places his hand on his heart*)

REDILLON. It's really nothing.

VATELIN. Nothing for you, but what about me? If it

were someone else's wife, it wouldn't matter—but when it's my lawful wife who deceives me—well, it's hard to bear.

REDILLON. Vatelin, will you allow me to tell you something in all sincerity?

VATELIN. Please do.

REDILLON. You are a nit-wit!

VATELIN. Do you think so?

REDILLON. I'm sure of it.

VATELIN. A deceived, unhappy nit-wit, then.

REDILLON. Oh, no, not at all. It's because you believe that nonsense, that you're a nit-wit. Now look here. One thing alone should have made you see the light.

VATELIN. What?

REDILLON. That note that said, "come to Rédillon's house and you will find me in the arms of my lover."

VATELIN. Well, she wrote it.

REDILLON. Of course she wrote it. But did you ever hear of a woman who went out to deceive her husband, and sent invitations to spectators?

VATELIN. I guess not.

REDILLON. You guess not. She sent you the note because she had a reason, and the reason was to make you jealous. But, as I heard the inspector say a few minutes ago, "this is the work of an angry woman, not an unfaithful wife."

VATELIN. Do you think so?

REDILLON. Everything points to it. First of all, staging it in my home.

VATELIN. Yes.

REDILLON. And that costume out of the Arabian Nights.

VATELIN. Yes.

ACT III THE FRENCH HAVE A WORD 123

REDILLON. And to choose Pontagnac whom she met only yesterday.

VATELIN. Yes.

REDILLON. I know I'm right because it was to me that she first offered the main role in the comedy – but I refused – and for good cause.

VATELIN. (*taking his hand*) Oh, my good friend.

REDILLON. And you fell in the trap. You're not a good hunter.

VATELIN. I'm a lawyer.

REDILLON. Of course.

VATELIN. Oh, I'm happy, I'm happy. (*HE is almost crying in both hands.*)

REDILLON. Joy brings tears.

(*At this moment LUCIENNE comes from rear room. SHE stops and sees sign from REDILLON that SHE should not speak. SHE stands quietly and listens.*)

VATELIN. How happy I am!

REDILLON. Come now – calm your joy.

VATELIN. Oh, my friend, go find my wife and tell her I love no one but her, and make her understand that she has the most faithful of husbands.

REDILLON. After your escapade last night?

VATELIN. Oh, do you think that escapade gave me any pleasure? I wish you could have been present at last night's ridiculous fiasco.

REDILLON. That would have been indiscreet.

VATELIN. Oh, you could have come. Everyone else was there. That Spanish witch with feet as big as a coal miner's was the cause of it all. Never before that one time in Spain did I ever deceive my wife. But I was gone a month and I was susceptible. I thought it was all over, and for me it was. But yesterday she came running after me. What a blackmailer she is. She threatened to make a scandal, and I was afraid to disturb my wife's happiness. But nothing at all happened between us last night. I swear.

REDILLON. It's too bad your wife can't hear you. (*HE sees that LUCIENNE is getting tearful as SHE moves down, behind VATELIN.*)

VATELIN. Yes, it's a pity she can't hear me. I think I could convince her. I think she would believe me. I would make myself so small, so repentant—she would see so much love in my eyes that she wouldn't have the strength to push me away, and I would hold out my hand to her and she would put her hand in mine, and I would hear her adorable voice say, "Crépin, I forgive you." (*VATELIN still has his hand out as HE sobs. REDILLON takes LUCIENNE's hand and puts it in VATELIN's.*)

LUCIENNE. Crépin, I forgive you.

VATELIN. (*rising*) Oh, you're wicked! You made me ill. (*HE falls sobbing into her arms.*) I adore you.

LUCIENNE. My dear husband.

REDILLON. (*who turns to hide his emotion*) I love both of you very much.

VATELIN. (*takes REDILLON's hand along with LUCIENNE's*) Our good friend.

(*THEY all hug each other.*)

INSPECTOR DUVAL. (*returning with others*) The report is finished if you would like to hear it.

VATELIN. Report? But there was no report. There is no need for a report. Tear it up.

DUPONT. But we just wrote it! Did you say to tear it up?
VATELIN. Of course, Inspectors, tear it up. (*HE takes one in each arm and leads them to rear.*)
DUVAL. But who is it that had us spinning like a weathercock?

(*VATELIN, with the 3 POLICEMEN, and PONTAGNAC disappear in hallway, rear.*)

REDILLON. (*to LUCIENNE*) Well?
LUCIENNE. Well?
REDILLON. It's all forgiven?
LUCIENNE. It's all forgiven.
REDILLON. And I'm finished?
LUCIENNE. Maybe not. You know what the fortune teller said. I would have two adventures in my life. One has passed, and the other one will be when I'm fifty-eight. Does that tempt you?
REDILLON. At fifty-eight?
LUCIENNE. That's not so old.
REDILLON. I'm sure you will still be charming at fifty-eight. But I'm sure I would be too tired.
LUCIENNE. Always!
REDILLON. Luckily for you!

(*VATELIN comes in followed by PONTAGNAC.*)

VATELIN. It's all settled. Now, as for you Pontagnac, I should be angry with you, but I have no hard feelings, and in proof, I invite you to dinner every Monday night. Will you be one of the regulars?
PONTAGNAC. Really? Why, of course. I'd be delighted.
VATELIN. It's a dinner for men only. That's the night

my wife visits her mother.

PONTAGNAC. (*realizing HE is being given a lesson*) With pleasure. (*HE walks downstage.*)

REDILLON. (*low to LUCIENNE*) If ever you need my services, please let me know the day before.

JEROME. (*coming in*) Is no one going to have lunch?

REDILLON. Of course we are. Do you have plenty of potatoes?

(*REDILLON, VATELIN, LUCIENNE go towards rear, arm in arm.*)

PONTAGNAC. (*facing audience*) I believe I was born to be the turkey. (*HE goes to rear, joining the others.*)

THE FRENCH HAVE A WORD FOR IT

END OF ACT THREE

END OF PLAY

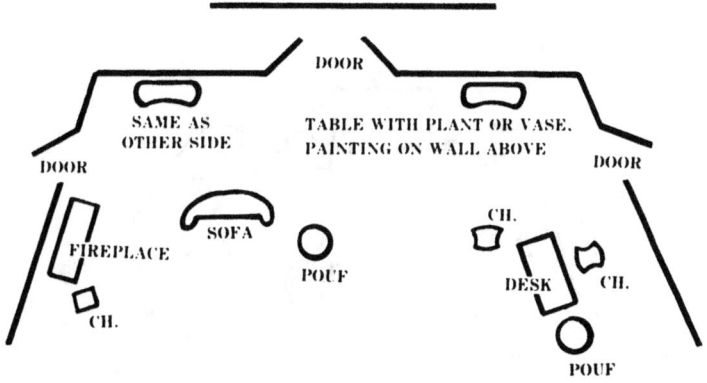

Set design — Act I

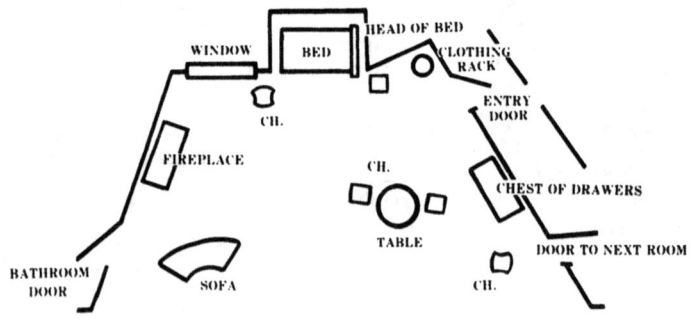

Set design — Act II

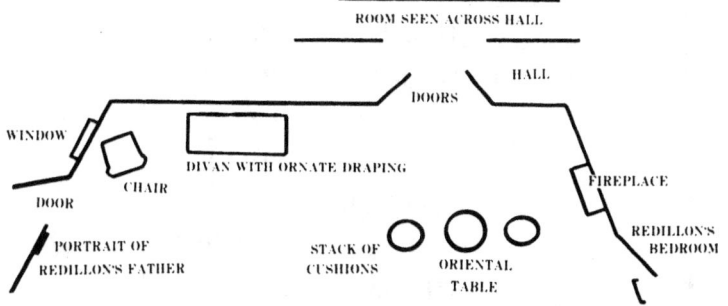

Set design — Act III

Also By
Georges Feydeau

13 RUE DE L'AMOUR

CAT AMONG THE PIGEONS

CHEMIN DE FER

A FITTING CONFUSION

A FLEA IN HER EAR

A GOWN FOR HIS MISTRESS

THE HAPPY HUNTER

HEY, CUT OUT THE PARADING AROUND STARK NAKED!

LADIES' MAN

THE LADY FROM MAXIM'S

LOOK AFTER LULU

NOT BY BED ALONE

ON THE MERRY-GO-WRONG

PARADISE HOTEL

THE PREGNANT PAUSE OR LOVE'S LABOR LOST

TAKE HER, SHE'S YOURS! OR
TILL DIVORCE DO US PART

SAMUELFRENCH.COM

OTHER TITLES AVAILABLE FROM SAMUEL FRENCH

THE DECORATOR
Donald Churchill

Comedy / 1m, 2f / Interior

Marcia returns to her flat to find it has not been painted as she arranged. A part time painter who is filling in for an ill colleague is just beginning the work when the wife of the man with whom Marcia is having an affair arrives to tell all to Marcia's husband. Marcia hires the painter a part time actor to impersonate her husband at the confrontation. Hilarity is piled upon hilarity as the painter, who takes his acting very seriously, portrays the absent husband. The wronged wife decides that the best revenge is to sleep with Marcia's husband, an ecstatic experience for them both. When Marcia learns that the painter/actor has slept with her rival, she demands the opportunity to show him what really good sex is.

"Irresistible."
– *London Daily Telegraph*

"This play will leave you rolling in the aisles....
I all but fell from my seat laughing."
– *London Star*

SAMUELFRENCH.COM

www.ingramcontent.com/pod-product-compliance
Lightning Source LLC
Chambersburg PA
CBHW070644300426
44111CB00013B/2247